5/9/13

Built.in Social

Essential
Social Marketing
Practices for
Every Small
Business

Jeff Korhan

WILEY

Cover image: Mouse Team © Marcello Bortolino/iStockphoto
Cover design: C. Wallace

Published by John Wiley & Sons, Inc., Hoboken, New Jersey.
Published simultaneously in Canada.

For general information about our other products and services, please contact
our Customer Care Department within the United States at (800) 762-2974,
outside the United States at (317) 572-3993 or fax (317) 572-4002.

Wiley publishes in a variety of print and electronic formats and by print-on-
demand. Some material included with standard print versions of this book
may not be included in e-books or in print-on-demand. If this book refers to
media such as a CD or DVD that is not included in the version you purchased,
you may download this material at http://booksupport.wiley.com. For more
information about Wiley products, visit www.wiley.com.

Library of Congress Cataloging-in-Publication Data:

Korhan, Jeff, 1957-
  Built-in social : essential social marketing practices for every small business /
Jeff Korhan.
    pages   cm
    Includes index.
  ISBN 978-1-118-52974-4 (hbk.); ISBN 978-1-118-63179-9 (ebk);
  ISBN 978-1-118-63189-8 (ebk); ISBN 978-1-118-63193-5 (ebk)
    1. Social marketing.   2. Small business.   I. Title.
  HF5414.K667 2013
  658.8'72—dc23
                                                    2012049075

Printed in the United States of America
10 9 8 7 6 5 4 3 2 1

To Ali and Zak—thank you for your honesty and inspiration.

Contents

CONTENTS

Preface

HOW BUILT-IN SOCIAL WILL HELP YOUR BUSINESS—A THREE-STEP PROCESS

This book is organized into three essential components or strategies, all of which build on your present marketing strategy, and of course, incorporate your process for closing sales.

First, we focus on the transformational shift in the business environment, why and how your business needs to adapt to it, and how a content marketing strategy is integral to accomplishing that online.

Then we get into the techniques of using social media well, by engaging with communities: getting to know them, helping to solve their problems, and ultimately building trust that can be converted into new business. It's a simple formula for helping people to know, like, and trust you and your business.

The final component of the three-step process shows you how to convert that trust into growing and sustaining your business, regardless of the economic conditions.

WHAT BUILT-IN SOCIAL WILL GIVE YOU

If you are a small business owner or work for a mainstream small business—this book is for you. Many of the books available on this subject miss the mark because they are not grounded in an understanding that comes from direct experience operating a mainstream small business, along with an understanding of how both social and media work.

For this reason, be prepared for fresh insights, honesty, and a few pleasant surprises. One of my objectives is to clarify and simplify so that you can start getting the results you have been expecting, but have nonetheless failed to achieve. In short, I hope to reignite your enthusiasm for this remarkable platform that is ideally suited to small businesses in local communities.

One of the reasons small businesses do not "get" social media is they see and hear so much about the technology, yet they miss the global understanding of how it works to accomplish practical business objectives. There are necessary skills you will have to develop to be successful, but they are not the ones that most businesses assume are important.

I will help you learn, in a relatively short period of time, what has taken me years of study and practice to develop—and that is grounded in decades of experience operating a mainstream small business. You'll learn how to use the social networks to engage and share your perspectives with the audiences for whom your solutions are most relevant. You'll better understand the role of search engines and how they influence buying behaviors, and most important, you will learn why content marketing is the most vital component of a viable social marketing strategy.

Ready to get started?

Introduction

YOU CAN DO THIS

After a successful decade as a corporate sales and marketing executive I was increasingly anxious to operate a business of my own. Months of research and study produced nothing more than anxiety. Then one day I just made a decision to indulge my love for plants and nature by starting a landscape business. What followed were two successful decades and thousands of practical lessons.

That business became a laboratory for testing ideas, and every time I made a breakthrough it seemed so obvious that I often wondered why there wasn't a manual of some kind where it was written down. Now there is. It turns out many of those lessons are just as relevant today, with the primary difference being how technology has introduced better methods and practices for getting results.

You don't need a marketing degree or to be technologically savvy to be successful with social marketing, although both are useful. More important is a basic understanding of business, the desire to help your customers, and a reliable

1

process to effectively engage them with your business in a meaningful way. *Built-In Social* gives you that process.

LESSONS FROM THE TRENCHES

There is a big difference between saying you are an entrepreneur and being one. When I was busy planning my landscape business I read a story about Jim Koch, the founder of The Boston Beer Company and brewer of Samuel Adams beer. He too was stuck in the planning stages of his entrepreneurial venture until his father pointed out one undeniable truth: you aren't in business if you don't have customers.

Those words instantly resonated with me, so I made a decision that Saturday summer morning to go out and get some customers. Not even having professional business cards, I wrote out my name, company name, and phone number on 3×5 index cards. I was now in business—almost. I just had to find those customers.

Back then you could still ring doorbells and get an attentive audience, so that's what I did. I drove to a neighborhood where there were plenty of newly constructed homes in need of landscaping. I vividly recall one conversation with a young attorney. He listened to suggestions and then gave me permission to engage my process. "Sounds good," he said. "So, I guess, go ahead and take measurements. You know, do whatever landscapers do."

What *do* landscapers do, I thought? I was like a deer in the headlights. Evidently, I hadn't quite thought everything through, but being pretty good at thinking on my feet, I assured him I would be back to take measurements later that day after I retrieved my measuring tools from my truck. Truth is, I didn't even own a truck.

Upon returning home, my wife greeted me with a question that was a reflection of my previous months of procrastination.

"I suppose you just drove around the neighborhood for the past three hours?" she asked. Proud to finally be in business, I replied with a smile, "No, I actually have three viable prospects and I don't know what the heck I'm doing!"

Lesson 1. You don't need to know everything about social media to get started. Just use good judgment and learn as you go.

In order to learn how landscape businesses operated, I revisited a few local suppliers that I had worked with when I landscaped my own home. They referred me to other contractors who were busy, and probably reluctant to introduce a new competitor to an already crowded market. Nevertheless, a few agreed to meet on job sites to show me how they were doing the work. What I learned was both fascinating and disturbing.

Everyone was doing it differently. The equipment, materials, and practices varied significantly from company to company. When I asked questions, the normal response was the other companies may be getting the work done, but they were not using the best methods.

Each of those small business owners were like different chefs who believed their secret sauce was what every customer should have. Their respective methods all had their merits, but were nevertheless consistently variable.

Lesson 2. Instead of copying other companies, seek to understand their methods to then develop better practices for marketing your business. The process described in *Built-In Social* will show you how.

Interestingly, there was one practice that all of these landscape businesses agreed on—advertising in the Yellow Pages. The Yellow Pages were without question the go-to source for finding businesses before the Internet and Google. I soon learned Yellow Page advertising was expensive. I couldn't believe how much money other companies were spending every month to be the one chosen by customers searching for a local landscape business.

To stand out in the Yellow Pages you needed to spend more for a larger and sometimes more colorful ad within your respective category. Since you were grouped together with all of your competitors, it was basically a game of who would be heard above the noise. Picture it as everyone trying to rank well for the same broad search terms, a game we all know has only a few winners.

Much like pay-per-click advertising enriches Google, the real winner with Yellow Page advertising is the one that owns the game. If you have ever been pressured to buy a vacation timeshare, you have a pretty good idea of the tactics used to sell Yellow Page advertising. Everything is predicated upon fear. The pitch is your company is going to fail if you do not spend heavily, and it worked nicely to create a neat little game with only one winner—the Yellow Pages.

> Lesson 3. The one that owns the game always has an advantage. Design your own game to assure your business success.

I didn't like that game so I designed my own. In fact, during the 20 years I owned that business I never once advertised in the Yellow Pages, just as I have never paid for clicks to my websites. Yet, I consistently rank quite well for my desired search terms. I chose to promote my landscape business in targeted community publications where the space was much more economical, giving me an opportunity to employ an entirely different approach—educating the community instead of emphatically announcing "Buy me." I appealed to reason by providing valid research and logical arguments to effectively help the community members become better buyers of landscape services, presumably my company's services.

Because there was so much confusion about best practices in our industry, I continued to do research and learn from anyone that would talk to me, after which I applied my own perspective based upon my intimate knowledge of the communities I served. Then I took that information to the people in the form of descriptive educational messages with calls to action.

For example, hand-pruning ornamental shrubs produces a healthier plant with an extended life expectancy. Many companies were using power shears because it reduces labor and requires less skill. Nobody ever explained to the customer that investing in a better method of pruning would preserve the natural habitat of their plants, thereby enhancing their beauty, extending their longevity, and saving money in the long run. The caption of my announcement was, "Are your plants being sheared to death?"

That particular promotion, accompanied by my crude hand drawing, was hardly sophisticated, but it got people's attention and the phone ringing. That was the goal—to get the phone ringing—and it worked. The homeowners only had to walk outside and look around to see that, in addition to their own landscape, there were many others that were not being well maintained.

I now recognize that I was practicing what is now commonly known as content marketing—using educational content to make a company more attractive to its desired customers by helping them solve problems—often problems they do not even know they have. Content marketing is now done digitally, and it is an essential component of your online marketing strategy.

> Lesson 4. Use educational content to get your community thinking, and for sharing with friends that influence their buying habits and behaviors.

As my business grew, we began to achieve awards and other forms of recognition for our work and community service. This helped us to get mentioned in local newspapers, which was a powerful validation by an influential third party, and something that also got the phone ringing. To encourage more of this, I made the effort to build relationships with local editors and freelance writers, offering to help them out with story ideas and interviews.

I learned that the media is always interested in a good story. While there were others nudging the press to write a story about their company, I went a step further and wrote the story for them. They didn't all get printed, but I quickly established myself as not only a subject matter expert, but one who could also take his expertise and make it interesting by wrapping a relevant story around it.

> Lesson 5. Learn to engage your community with interesting stories about your business. Once in awhile an influential connection will share your story and it will go viral.

Today, influence is no longer localized among enterprises and media outlets as it was back then. It is dispersed among millions of people and organizations that have learned how to use social media to engage a community. Celebrities clearly have broad influence, but across the globe regular people like you and me have specialized influence because we are subject matter experts, something social media is amplifying.

Content creates the potential for engaging a community by giving it something to talk about. This is the element for attracting attention to your business. This was true with newspapers and other traditional media channels, and it is true today. The only difference is traditional media outlets are being outmaneuvered by digital ones that also happen to have a global reach. Blogs, in particular, are considered to be valid news sources, and therefore one of the most vital online marketing tools available to every business, large or small.

Just as there were few companies educating their communities when I started my business, so it is today. This is the opportunity that is yours for the taking.

While blogging and social media have matured in many ways, they are still ripe with opportunity. One reason for this is that the Yellow Pages mindset is still alive and well. Many businesses are using social media to be heard, yet all they are really doing is adding to the noise level.

That's not how social marketing works. You get results by helping your community, being a resource, solving problems, staying connected and engaging whenever possible, and occasionally asking the community to buy from you.

The truth is, your community will want to buy from you if you properly establish your business as qualified, willing to help, and likeable. All of this can be readily accomplished by designing your business practices around the consistent needs of the consumers you want to attract and convert into customers.

> The final lesson is the same as the first. Recognize the opportunity for using digital media to be more socially engaged with the communities you serve.

PART ONE

Attraction: Your Essential Content Marketing Strategy

CHAPTER 1

How the Social Web Works

As new technologies are integrated with the growing body of social data, you can expect search capabilities to rise to breathtaking levels.

In the classic film *The Wizard of Oz*, Dorothy receives the following instructions on how to get to the magical land of Oz from Glinda, the good witch of the North: "It's always best to start at the beginning, and all you do is follow the Yellow Brick Road." Seems simple enough; start at the beginning, and follow a reliable path. Yet that sound advice is apparently uncommon when it comes to launching a company's social marketing program. This is usually due to the fact that many people don't know where the true beginning is—or the reliable path that follows from it.

The Internet was originally designed to connect multiple computers so they could communicate with each other and share information. As more computers were connected and more information was shared, it became necessary to make that information discoverable, which meant the Internet had to be searchable. The web as we know it today is driven by search.

This is why you should always consider the impact of search when planning and implementing your online marketing—because search drives the web. Learn how it really works, trust it to guide your efforts, and you will control your destiny.

One of the greatest mistakes businesses make with their online marketing is to downplay or completely disregard how search will impact their results. *Built-In Social* provides information that will open your eyes to basic principles that have long been shrouded in mystery by Internet marketing experts. After spending years in the dark myself, I began a quest to learn the truth. This book is the result of that quest, and the truth that I discovered will liberate your social marketing efforts.

Built-In Social teaches you essential practices that will help you become adept at achieving higher search engine rankings for your websites. The web was indeed designed to make it easier for people to discover informational content—predominantly for research purposes. Of course, search queries have evolved to deliver much more than web pages; they now include images, videos, and the burgeoning mountain of social commentary that is transforming how the web works, and therefore how you should be using it.

On that note—let's get started with how to best position your business marketing to take full advantage of this phenomenon that is completely changing how business is done.

SOCIAL MARKETING IS A PROCESS

Social media marketing—now more appropriately known simply as social marketing—is a strategic process designed to make a business and its products and services more attractive to buyers. Of course, this has always been the goal of modern marketing. The significant difference today is that much of this is accomplished digitally—and in order to start properly, you must respect the vital role that search plays in the process, and how content marketing relates to that. Only then are you equipped to use social media well. This is the mistake businesses make—jumping into social media without a plan or thorough understanding of how it will generate sales revenue. When you make social media marketing a checkbox, you miss the message of this book—it has to be built into the fabric of your business structure, because it is similarly influencing the habits and behaviors of the communities your business serves.

As Figure 1.1 shows, the social marketing process is a simple three-step progression that begins with useful and valuable content that attracts the attention of buyers, followed by using social media to engage them further to build relationships and earn trust, resulting in new business that is predominantly accomplished in the real world with direct selling.

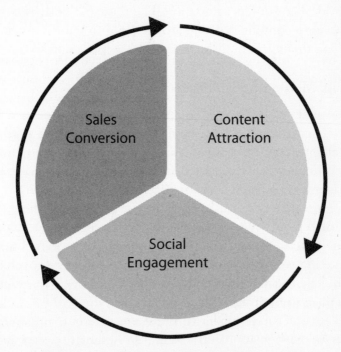

Figure 1.1 The Social Marketing Process©

Marketing Always Starts with Attraction

The early days of modern marketing focused on advertising. These were the glory days of Madison Avenue, when perception was everything. Now choice has replaced perception—and informational content is an essential component that helps consumers make better choices.

In order to make your brand attractive today, you need more than slick advertising; you have to answer questions and solve problems. This is the purpose of your content marketing—and however you position it, you should design it to create value. Value is essential in this economy, which is quite a departure from the days when marketers "sold the sizzle instead of the steak" to attract buyers.

Your content marketing challenge is simple: learn what your ideal customers value most. Then use that understanding to develop content that will attract them to your business by helping them accomplish more of what they want to do.

Social Media Engages Buyers

Consumers now have a voice—and that voice plays a big part in determining the value of your brand. The truth is, for all practical purposes, your customers own your brand. Marketing starts with attraction, then the next logical step is engagement—which social media does especially well.

Unfortunately, not many businesses readily understand this. Consider your own business: do you expect to go straight from attraction to a sale, just because that is how traditional marketing worked? While that may occasionally be possible, it is unlikely, much as it would be unlikely to expect to progress straight into marriage after the first date.

Use your social media to build engagement, and remain open to new relationships. Make it a point to learn about your community and how you can help. Social marketing is a process designed to build the trust necessary to be relevant in any economy—but especially one that is strongly influenced by the collective voice of consumers.

Sales Converts Engagement into New Business

You know your sales process; it's often one that you intuitively developed to successfully grow your business. It should ideally be written out in a step-by-step fashion so that everyone on your team knows how it works. This is also necessary to make sure that your team is clear about its vital importance for bringing home the business that your content marketing and social media engagement have rightfully earned.

Having a well-designed sales process not only gives your team confidence; it also does the same for your prospective customers by letting them know, in no uncertain terms, that you have a plan for taking them where they want to go. The best way to refine your sales process is to review your greatest successes. Then break down all of the steps you followed to make them happen. You will discover patterns—some of which you may have eliminated that once served you well.

The cycle of attraction, engagement, and conversion are elements that comprise a simple yet reliable formula for social marketing success. They provide a structure that works because it starts at the logical beginning and progressively builds from there. That beginning starts with search.

SEARCH DRIVES THE WEB

Understanding Google's primary objective—to deliver the most relevant results as quickly as possible for every search query—is essential, because that mission is something from which the search giant has never wavered. The challenge for businesses that want to be more visible online is to learn the nuances of exactly what information search engines consider to be most relevant and why. You can then start actively creating it in such a way that leaves "a trail of breadcrumbs" back to your business by way of searchable keyword phrases.

As a point of convention, when referring to search engines I will nearly always mention Google because it is universally recognized as the leader. Google controls roughly two-thirds of search in the United States and even more in other parts of the world. Nearly all of the remaining balance is handled by Bing, the Microsoft search engine that also drives Yahoo! and Facebook search.

In addition to search on the open web, you also want to keep in mind that several of the respective social networks—including LinkedIn, Google+, and Twitter—are all internally searchable, and to some degree on the open web, too. Facebook is the exception; its search capabilities have been reserved for targeting Facebook advertising—a task that the site accomplishes with amazing accuracy. Although, that is changing with the introduction of Graph Search, a feature that promises to make Facebook more "open and connected." Nevertheless, you should know that, for the most part, what happens within Facebook stays there—much to Google's disappointment.

The Game of Search

Despite its dominance, it is important to remember that Google isn't the only player in the game of search. Facebook, LinkedIn, Twitter, and other sites are all hungry for content, too. They want high quality material that people will find entertaining, will help them solve problems, and will generally attract attention to their sites. Since you want interested buyers to visit your sites, your role in this game is learning how to help them—so they can help you in return. And they will do that by linking back to your original content.

Learning the game of search engine optimization, or SEO, is a vital component of any successful social marketing strategy. Many experts would have you believe that it is a complicated science—and indeed it is, at its highest level. Yet, this is true with any endeavor. But becoming proficient with search doesn't need to be complicated; it just requires you undertake a practice of learning what your customers find most useful, creating it for them, and helping them locate it using the social networks.

You will find that it's really not that difficult to get good results from SEO if you employ a proven process and consistently implement it.

The business of search generates billions of dollars in advertising revenue for the respective players. That is what is at stake for Google, Facebook, Twitter, and the others—and why they are eager for your active involvement. They have a job to do: serving their users with useful information. Your job is quite simple—give them what they want so they will lead those users to your business.

SEARCH ENGINE OPTIMIZATION FOR REGULAR PEOPLE

Search optimization is simple when you learn to think like regular people that respond best to simple language. And regular people are engaged by straightforward headlines, descriptive subheadings, and keyword phrases highlighted in bold letters. Creating web copy that follows these guidelines respects the short attention spans of the majority of individuals—including your customers—who want you to get to the point quickly. For example, "How to Protect Your Facebook Account from Hackers" is the title of an article I wrote that has earned thousands of shares—and it continues to accumulate more views every day—and that is a direct result of the no-nonsense headline with content that delivers on its promise. (Go to the Appendix for a link to this article and other online resources.)

Once you have the attention of your audience, you can then use original stories to humanize your message. But don't forget to keep the stories short. Offer bite-sized paragraphs that allow for quick and easy consumption, and use images and videos to descriptively tell your story. Everyone prefers to learn in their own unique way, so it always helps to provide multimedia options for ensuring that people not only receive your message, but also understand it clearly. Also, remember that Google is reading your story, too—and looking for relevant keywords that provide clues to the content of your message and its ideal audience.

Keyword Selection Simplified

Keyword selection for SEO is a process of using words in your web copy that most people in a mainstream community would use to search for a business like yours. You have to think middle of the road, like a regular person. This is a test of how well you understand your customer—which you may discover is not as well as you think you do.

Of course, there's an easy way to determine what your customers want and the words they use to express it: ask them. When I owned my landscape business and was just beginning to learn about keyword optimization for our website, I decided to survey my customers to find out which words they would use to describe us. It turned out to be a wise move—one that I highly recommend, and that's easy to implement using online survey tools such as SurveyMonkey.com, online form builder Wufoo.com, or Google Docs forms. I gave them a list of words from which to choose and asked them to select the ones that they would use to search for a company like ours.

The phrases included terms like landscape contractor, landscape architect, landscape designer, and landscaper, among others. Our customers overwhelmingly chose landscaper—not a particularly flattering term that we were especially excited about featuring in our content. However, it was what they used. And since we realized we could either feed our egos or rank better for search results, we chose the latter.

Optimizing for landscaper—instead of the other common industry phrases we had been using—moved our site from page seven to page one for a local search within 60 days. One month later, we had the top two listings on the first page. This was not only exciting, it was our first clue that very few companies were optimizing their sites, or knew how to do it well. The second insight came after I sold the business. Even though our website hadn't been updated in nearly three years, it still ranked on page one for our desired search terms.

You should know that I accomplished all of this in a period of just a few months with no training other than a few decades of working with real customers. You cannot underestimate that experience. Assuming you similarly have extensive experience working with your customers, you have the most essential quality for making SEO work for your business: you know your customers and what they want. The only other help you need is a little technical guidance—and that you are learning here.

Most websites are not properly optimized because most webmasters are technicians—not people who understand your business as well as you do. Use your experience and expertise to help them do their job well. Many business owners with 10, 20, and 30 or more years of experience are impressed with what their younger employees can do with technology—but it really should be the other way around. This technology is useless when it's not grounded in time-tested business practices.

Virtually any keyword optimization effort that you develop from your sound understanding of your core customer and company mission will be beneficial, because the majority of businesses—including your competitors—are doing nothing at all. Sure, they may be paying for clicks or running ads, but that is not sustainable. The monster that is Google needs to be fed. You can feed it dollars and get modest results, or you can give it fresh meat—original content that it will devour and then come back to you for more. Once Google finds a valuable source of original content in your business, you've built a bridge—one that is that much easier to cross the next time around.

In addition to using your experience and instincts when choosing keywords, there are online services such as Wordtracker.com and (Google) Adwords.com that will tell you what people are universally searching for. Just keep in mind these tools examine the entire web, whereas you may only be interested in your local community, and there is no substitute for local knowledge when it comes to doing that well. You can of course use the tools—but trust your gut, too. One of the most effective tools you can use is a simple Google search. Enter a search query, and as you type, Google will serve up—in a prioritized fashion—the most commonly searched terms for that keyword phrase. (See Figure 1.2.) Use your expertise to judge how relevant those terms may be.

FRESHNESS AND AUTHORITY FOR RELEVANCE AND INFLUENCE

Google has traditionally used a "freshness factor" as a measure of relevancy to determine the best search results. In other words, the newest information is given greater consideration for being more relevant. This makes sense, because the most recent news is clearly likely to be more relevant (a factor that also explains the precipitous decline of print newspapers and related publications in a world that has largely gone digital).

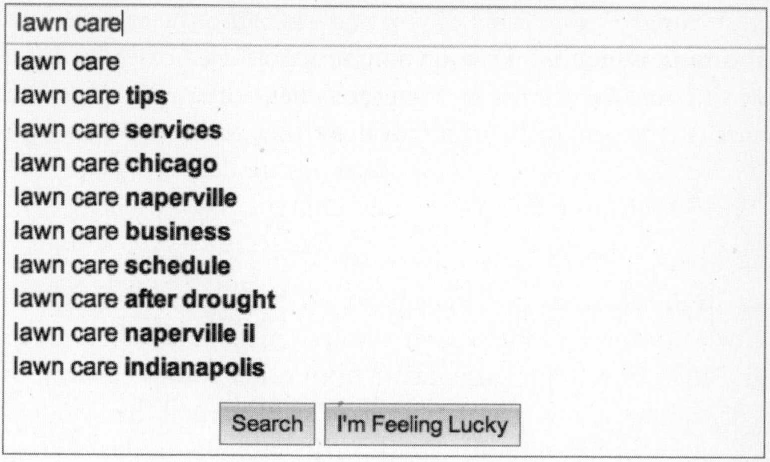

```
lawn care|
lawn care
lawn care tips
lawn care services
lawn care chicago
lawn care naperville
lawn care business
lawn care schedule
lawn care after drought
lawn care naperville il
lawn care indianapolis
                      [ Search ] [ I'm Feeling Lucky ]
```

Figure 1.2   Google Search for Lawn Care

The second key consideration for ranking search results is the authority of the news source. Traditional media outlets such as newspapers and magazines once held massive influence, because they were few in number and had exclusive access to news that the general public eagerly anticipated. Today, the general public serves as both the news and its source.

There are millions of blogs today, many of which have more influence than traditional news sources such as *Forbes* or even *USA Today*. This democratization of media presents a significant opportunity for every small business. Social media has made it possible for a single person to become influential literally overnight. Now authority and influence is not consolidated within institutions, or even among celebrities and power brokers. It's everywhere, and it's specific.

You and your business may have a great deal of influence within your industry and the communities you serve. Thus, if someone is searching for the products and services your company provides, your influence will be weighted accordingly—especially if you are leveraging factors such as location, which is an undeniable source of authority for local businesses. We discuss in Chapter 7 why businesses large and small are trying to be more local, even hyperlocal.

The Freshness Factor

In early 2011, Google implemented the first of their series of freshness updates. This update to their search algorithm (formula for ranking search results) effectively killed websites that were repurposing data from other sources instead of creating fresh and relevant content. This opened the window of opportunity wide for every small business leader willing to digitize the knowledge and expertise that presently resides within their gray matter—thereby allowing Google to index and share it with those who are searching for businesses with that specific expertise.

Good quality information that helps your community will never go out of style. This is what we call evergreen content—information that will be just as relevant tomorrow as it is today. So, what makes it fresh? Quite simply, your timely perspective—one that is relevant to your industry, community, and customers.

Authority Is Influence

In the 1970s television commercials for stock brokerage firm E. F. Hutton, the catchphrase "When E. F. Hutton Talks—People Listen" was used to position the firm as a respected authority in the financial services industry—something that a business can earn over a period of time with a proven track record.

Authority is why Google considers me to be influential when it comes to social media for small business. Why? Because I have earned my "author-ity" by authoring and publishing content that has earned inbound links from other blogs that publish portions of my work and link back to me. Those inbound links are signals of authority to Google—digital validations or votes of confidence.

Thus, in addition to creating and publishing fresh content, your business has to use your social media to promote it and earn those inbound links. The key is to do this in service to others, who will in turn acknowledge the value of your work by linking to it.

Two of the most common mistakes that business owners make with their social marketing are failing to properly promote their content—and over-promoting it, sometimes referred to on Twitter as "hogging the stream." Consider how often you would watch a television station that was 100 percent advertising. If you have been over-promoting your work, take a step back and rebuild your reputation as a valued contributor to your social communities.

FACEBOOK AND THE WISDOM OF FRIENDS

Search advertising revenue is what makes Google, Facebook, LinkedIn, YouTube, and Twitter free for users. How they accomplish that varies, and the Facebook model in particular is one that businesses should learn. More on how this works in Chapter 4, when we examine the major social networks in more detail.

As you now know, Google's mission is to deliver the most relevant results for anyone performing a search within its platform. Thus, Google is always clear about who their customer is: any person performing a search query, regardless of whether they're performing that search for personal or business reasons.

When Google focuses on providing the best user experience, they are serving everyone equally. In order to make a profit, Google employs a business strategy for delivering favorable results for both organic (driven purely by the value of the content) and paid search results—both of which are designed to be the most relevant results for a search query.

Contrast this with Facebook. Let's say that you and I are Facebook users (which we likely both are). Facebook users are not necessarily their customers—and that compromises the value of the user experience for both users and business customers that pay for advertising. In the early days, before Facebook launched their advertising revenue model, it was designed to create the best experience for networking. Now everything is designed for the true customer—businesses that want to connect with users.

One of the likely reasons that individual users are limited to 5,000 Facebook friends is because Facebook wants to encourage anyone desiring a greater presence to migrate their personal Facebook experience to a page. This compels them to assume the role of a personality or business, one that is encouraged to purchase advertising to stay engaged with their fans. This is presumably why Facebook is better searchable within the context of targeting specific users with ads—with Graph Search for users providing limited results from profile data and relationships.

This is unfortunate because with over one billion users actively sharing, Facebook is building a storehouse of valuable contextual data that insiders have appropriately named "the wisdom of friends." When it comes to making buying decisions, our friends' recommendations are arguably one of the most important considerations—because they take a variety of factors including social influences, location, and direct experience from trusted sources into account.

While Facebook CEO Mark Zuckerberg has stated they could "create a web that's smarter, more social, more personalized, and more semantically aware," that reality has been a long time coming, despite years of anticipation. The truth is that not only is Facebook only partly searchable, the user experience is filtered for everyone who uses it, including businesses.

As stated previously, Facebook takes this approach in order to encourage businesses to invest in advertising and promoted posts to reach a wider audience. Yet even this has been met with mixed results. For instance, while they still invest a portion of their marketing budget with Facebook, General Motors cancelled a $10 million Facebook advertising campaign in 2012 due to lack of results, with Mark Cuban later responding in kind with the Facebook marketing of his 70-plus companies. The message is clear—evaluate your results.

My clients have generally received mixed results from Facebook advertising, ranging from exceptional to marginal. The problem is there is only so much room in the Facebook stream, just as there is only room for so many Super Bowl ads. So, while some Facebook ads work exceptionally well, there are others that may not get served at all. Of course, there is no cost incurred if that happens. That said, as long as the pricing remains reasonable, it is worth experimenting with these ads to build more traffic to your Facebook page, with the hopes that someday you will also be able to better search Facebook for valuable insights on your customers.

SOCIAL GRAPHS—THE SECRET YOU NEED TO KNOW

In the real world, you have relationships with objects as well as with people. For example, the car you drive reflects your personality and tendencies. Minivans suggest practicality, convertibles a love of freedom, and tinted windows clearly indicate a desire for privacy. That's in the real world.

Now consider that the web works exactly the same way, except that everything has to be accomplished digitally. Your digital relationships with people and objects provide clues about you. Objects in the digital world are videos, images, and just about any other type of searchable content—including everything within your social media. All of this content collectively makes up something called your social graph: a digital representation of who you are as told by your personal information, connections, and associated content that you have created and shared.

Think of these social graphs as digital maps that help to create alignment online. To get a visual of social graphs, imagine a three-dimensional matrix of horizontal and vertical lines, comprised of mostly empty space. Every point of intersection on that matrix is a potential connection point or node. When you make a social connection with another person, object, or company, you create a permanent node that makes the matrix more descriptive. Every node is a relationship that tells a story—your story. And the more active you are on a given social network, the more nodes you have and the more completely your social graph reflects who you are in real life.

As a practical matter, you want your business to have a descriptive social graph to create better alignment with it and your ideal customers—the people who are searching for a company like yours. Just as you have to give Google what it wants if you expect to rank well in search on the open web, you have to do the same for Facebook, LinkedIn, and every other social network where you want a stronger presence.

The term social graph was first used in reference to Facebook, and is now literally represented in its Graph Search feature; however, it applies to every social network, and even related platforms such as Google and Amazon. Digital graphing on sites such as Amazon would more accurately be described as "interest graphs" since they align buyers of one product with potentially related products. Google prefers the term "knowledge graph" regarding search. Don't get hung up on the terminology; just recognize the power behind these digital social graphs for accomplishing your social marketing objectives.

The Facebook Open Graph

When Facebook launched sweeping changes to their platform on April 21, 2010, social graphs were suddenly thrust into the spotlight, predominantly due to privacy concerns. That's when Mark Zuckerberg coined a new term—Open Graph. The objective of Facebook's Open Graph is to integrate its users' social graphs on other sites with their identity on Facebook. Facebook accomplishes this through something called the Facebook API, which you know as the familiar Facebook Like button.

When you "Like" a Facebook page on an outside site that has embedded the Facebook Like feature, you are instantly connected with everyone else who has liked that site. Every Facebook Like connects and extends your reach into these communities, which tells Facebook more about who you are, your interests, and how you are associated with others.

As all of our social graphs are merged, they become mutually more descriptive and complete. This is why it's important to be actively engaged on the social networks—both on a personal and professional level. Doing so allows you to manage your destiny by building your social graphs to connect the dots to new friends and business opportunities.

How Social Graphs Tell a Story

Bill Gates is credited with noting in 1996 that "content is king"—and at that time, he was right. However, that was before social networking changed the game of search to what it is today—one where social context is equally important.

As your messaging or content on the social web is shared, it gathers context and builds nodal relationships that tell a story. Once you understand this, you can more effectively enhance your social graph by creating useful content that favorably represents who you are and what you do best in all of your personal and professional roles.

Context not only tells us who you are, it also suggests who you are not. When you are open and authentic, you are likely to attract what you really want. Any company that tries to be all things to all people will necessarily have to work harder at filtering leads and inquiries. Thus, when a company is clear about its identity and mission and reinforces that with content shared on the social networks, it tends to attract buyers that the business can serve well.

Social graphs are predictors of human behavior. We are creatures of habit who are more likely to behave in the future as we have in the past. Conditioned patterns seldom change—and social graphs accurately reflect that. While it is technically not necessary to understand social graphs in order to network effectively, developing this understanding is invaluable for adapting to changes as this technology evolves.

Why Social Search Is a Game Changer

Google has hundreds of online properties, including Gmail, YouTube, and Google+, but its core business is, and presumably will always be, search advertising. That is how it makes the lion's share of its revenue, and that alone provides clues for understanding how to use the web to your advantage.

You may have already noticed that socially shared content is rising to the top of your Google search results. So if you want to earn higher Google rankings, you not only need to be creating high-quality content, you must also be actively encouraging people to share this content on the social networks.

Why is there now so much emphasis on social content? Well, for one thing, there's so much of it. Google can't ignore the fact that people are creating social content at a breathtaking pace. And because search is all about content, Google has to go where the action is. Add to that the richness of social data and you have a game changer—one in which context is king.

As new technologies are integrated with this growing body of social data, you can expect search capabilities to rise to breathtaking levels, providing timelier, more accurate, and more personal search results.

What This Means for Business

In late 2010 at the Web 2.0 Summit, Mark Zuckerberg made the profound statement that every industry will have to redesign itself around the influences of social media in the coming years. This means that every leading business will have to do the same.

Imagine a web that has perfect access to information—a social web that is a digital copy of your physical world. That nearly impossible-to-imagine reality is here today. Every piece of data that is added to every social graph makes the entire system more intelligent. And the more the system knows, the more discerning it will be. Think about what that means for your business, and how you should be preparing it for a future that may already be here now.

Try This: Select Your Keywords

You can think of keywords simply as the language of the web—what consumers and businesses are using to get what they desire from a web search.

What are the keywords your buyers are using?

- Have a conversation with a few of your customers. After you reconnect, casually ask them what words they would use to search for a company like yours.

- Write everything down. You may be surprised what you learn.

- Start by using these key words and phrases to optimize your social media profiles for search.

- Now go back to some of your recently published content and do the same—especially recent blog posts and website content.

- Make it a habit to be laser-focused on using these keywords whenever you publish online, while also noticing which keywords generate more traffic.

CHAPTER 2

Designing Your Business
Around Social

*It is arguably more important to understand the influences of social
media than to necessarily be using it.*

Consider how and why customers choose your company
over others. It is likely the result of their consideration of countless logical and emotional factors that are influenced by those
closest to them. People rarely make important buying decisions
without at least considering the opinions of their family, friends,
or respected business associates. They know that the approval or
acknowledgment of others provides valuable context for making decisions that are less likely to lead to the all too common
post-purchase phenomenon known as buyer's remorse.

Social influence colors the hard facts, thereby shaping them
to sometimes significantly affect the outcome of the decision-
making process. This is why experienced sales professionals
will always try to work with buyers in an environment that
gives buyers the freedom to share their influences, thereby

helping the business to offer solutions that strike a balance among those needs, wants, and desires.

APPLE RETAIL STORES

Anyone who has purchased a computer online or over the telephone has probably experienced a similar sense of frustration. You are able to order one that meets your exact specifications, if only you had more technological know-how or a trusted advisor to guide you through the process. Additionally, you are making an important and significant investment without the ability to even once test drive the technology. This is a lousy way to buy a computer—or really, any piece of technology.

The brilliance of Apple retail stores is they make the process of buying a computer a social experience—one in which you can see and touch the devices while also sharing and collaborating with friends and other informed buyers in the store. You are free to come and go as many times as you wish until you are comfortable with your preparedness to make a decision. The result: people show up in great numbers just to explore. They enjoy and learn from the experience, which thereby gives them the confidence to buy.

It's not that computers were not sold in stores before Apple came along; they were. However, the environment was anything but social. There was usually only one model available to examine; the lighting was marginal at best; and, most significantly, there were no trained representatives ready to answer the customers' every question. Apple revolutionized this process, which is a key reason why their stores that boast exceptional sales per square foot of retail space are a model for retailers in every industry.

The success of Apple retail stores is a perfect example of how to design a business around social—that is, around the customer and how they ideally want to buy. It is a simple concept that you can adapt and apply to your business, whether you are selling physical products or services. If you can make the experience of buying from your company social, you will make it much more relevant for the business environment—one that is being profoundly impacted by social media's unprecedented influences.

The fact is, human beings are hard-wired to engage. This is why social influences have always been pertinent to buying decisions, and why smart marketers are tapping into their power by designing their businesses around them. It's a new approach that differs from the traditional mindset of selling to buyers. We now realize how crucial it is to collaborate with buyers as equal partners in what may—or may not—lead to a commercial transaction.

One thing that makes buying decisions stressful is people are afraid of making a mistake—one that they will hear about again and again from their social influencers. This is especially true in the risk-averse economy we are now experiencing. People still rely on their friends for recommendations; however, they are now validating those recommendations with online research, which includes commentary from the social networks. Thus, when you design a business around social, you have to account for the information available through the social networks, and how those channels are shaping offline buying behaviors.

Because my landscape business focused on residential customers, we were careful to not only encourage but also require spouses and influential partners to be involved in as many steps of the buying process as possible. We even had a room with toys and drawing materials to entertain children so that parents could feel free to take as much time as necessary to consider the various options.

We offered all of this well before social media became part of the picture. Today, we would go a step further to share whatever was necessary for them to feel confident that they were making a wise decision to even consider meeting with our company. For retail businesses, this could be as simple as sharing a video that captures the magic of the in-store experience, and why it is a better option than taking a chance of making an online purchase that ultimately proves to be more expensive.

INFLUENCERS ARE YOUR ALLIES

One of my favorite and longtime landscape customers, named Bob, began our relationship by informing me that wherever he has lived, his home raised the bar with respect to new standards for beautiful landscaping. He informed me that his goal with his new home was to create a showplace whose beauty would be appreciated by his family, friends, and neighbors alike. Of course, we loved the idea—and we enthusiastically worked together to make that happen.

Although Bob was pleased with our work, he was not necessarily delighted. This was something we learned when he informed us—after 10 years of working together—that he was entertaining designs from competing companies in addition to ours. While this came as a surprise to us, it should not have. Every business that is at risk of losing a customer usually knows in their gut they are not hitting the mark, and this was no exception. The challenge is acting on that impulse before it's too late.

Bob was a tough negotiator who tested our limits, and we respected that. He stretched our capabilities to make our company better for all of our customers. Though we knew that we had a 50–50 chance, at best, for keeping his business, this particular project would prove to be the ultimate test.

Our team set to work pulling together our most creative ideas for a design that would regain his trust and loyalty. We also made some important changes worth noting. Up until this point, Bob had persuaded us to stray from our proven process in a number of ways, including meeting at his home instead of at our offices as we did with every other customer. This time, however, we affirmed our desire to meet at our offices so that we could involve all of our team and better focus. From the moment he and his wife walked into the door, there was a different energy in the room. They arrived well dressed, as if they were ready for a show—and that is exactly what we gave them.

Our design was everything they had hoped for and more. They were indeed delighted, and we were both excited and relieved. Then Bob—always the consummate negotiator—asked the price. That's when I explained what I suspected he already knew; it was more than twice his budget. It was of course very risky to present a project that far over the budget; however, we did so based on a decade-long knowledge of our customer, along with the awareness that this could be our last shot at retaining their business. We knew what would make them happy, but had always respected the budget in the past.

Without hesitation, Bob turned to his wife and asked if this was what she wanted. She not only said yes, she also elaborated on specifically why. We had never seen anything like this before. Bob usually controlled the negotiations by focusing nearly exclusively on price. He then looked me squarely in the eye and said the magic words: "Let's do it." To be honest, even we were a little surprised at how easily we arrived at a deal. There were more negotiations later, but that was just something we expected in working with Bob.

We knew from that first meeting 10 years earlier that what Bob and his wife really wanted was an eye-popping environment they would be proud to share with their friends. The landscape that we ultimately delivered included elaborate water features and extensive stonework, along with plantings that transformed a small backyard with a view into a special place where you felt like you were on vacation every day of the week.

When the project was completed, our key managers and I sat down on the terrace to enjoy a glass of lemonade with Bob and his wife. It was very relaxing. Everything looked, and most important, felt right about our renewed relationship with Bob and his wife. We talked for about an hour, laughing about some of the challenges we encountered during this substantial project. Then, unexpectedly, Bob's wife stepped inside for a few minutes. What happened after that I'll never forget. He smiled broadly while leaning forward to whisper, "You guys nailed it; she loves it!"

By shifting our approach from selling to collaborative problem solving, we reinvented our relationship with our customer, while also discovering the power of influencers. There are a lot of well-intentioned Bob's out there, but you will never make them happy if you underestimate their social influencers—who, in this case, was someone very close to home.

Designing your business around social requires that you understand that business today is no longer about selling to buyers. Rather, it focuses on working with them in collaborative ways to create solutions that are even better than anything they have imagined. Another interesting outcome of this particular experience is that we began working almost exclusively with Bob's wife on day-to-day matters. The true decision maker had now been revealed.

Businesses can use social media to engage with both customers and those who influence their decisions. Every one of us has influencers, because we all have a circle of friends whose opinions we value. That "wisdom of friends" is what gives every one of these networks the potential for shaping the decisions of your customers. To paraphrase author Guy Kawasaki, most of us are not somebody who is well-known. Yet, everybody is a somebody within his or her circle of friends—no matter how small the circle. Thanks to the power of the social networks, the influence of nobodies is amplified—thereby making nobodies the new somebodies.

Get to know the nobodies in your communities; you will learn new perspectives and discover fresh ideas that will transform your business.

THE INFLUENCE OF SOCIAL MEDIA

There is a notable quote by communications theorist Marshall McLuhan: "The medium is the message." This statement suggests that media's influences are just as relevant, if not more important, than the actual messages it delivers. This certainly applies to the new social media that are contributing to the democratization of all forms of media.

To understand how to operate a business in this social media–influenced environment is to recognize and appropriately respond to social media's humanizing qualities. It is a fact that it is arguably more important to understand the influences of social media than to necessarily be using it.

While many companies are busy adding social media to their marketing practices, they are not fully understanding the magic that makes it work: its humanizing qualities that make your business more approachable. For the most part, businesses are simply adding a social layer to their marketing, like a fresh coat of paint. What they should be doing instead is baking the qualities of social into every aspect of the business—from operations to sales, marketing, and customer service.

This is especially true for small business, where effective social marketing realistically calls for owners and management team members to become directly involved. After all, these are the individuals with the decades of vital experience for capably processing and responding to the engagement that new media technologies make possible. To delegate those interactions to lower-level employees risks compromising what social media does best: humanizing your business to make it more likeable, trustworthy, and therefore more attractive to the new customers that have yet to learn about it.

SOCIAL CREATES EXPECTATIONS

What would you think if you visited your favorite store and found it closed at a time when it is normally open? Over time, customers develop expectations, and one of them is that your business is open, ready, and willing to serve.

If you operate a small business, you understand this. You open and close on time and follow a number of other standard business practices.

A new expectation is that your business is friendly. This is a by-product of our social media influenced world. In many ways, social media creates new expectations of businesses.

Here are five of the more relevant expectations that are now becoming part of the fabric of the business environment—one in which every business will have to adapt to if it expects to enjoy continued relevance and growth.

1. *Visibility.* We are living in a period in which a business without an online presence is likely to be considered irrelevant by many consumers. Whereas customers will

perceive a company with an active social presence to be engaged with the community and openly prepared for more business.

2. *Authenticity.* Customers want to have a relationship with your company; they want to know what's going on behind the scenes. They are curious, and you have to feed that curiosity in order for those relationships to flourish.

3. *Accessibility.* The web gives everyone more access to people, companies, and causes. This ease of attaining information has conditioned consumers to expect to have open access to your business—and especially with you, if you are the owner or one of its leaders.

4. *Community.* It is no longer possible to be successful without a meaningful relationship with the communities you serve, as communities are the new markets. They equally serve the needs of businesses and the people within them. This is why locally engaged companies have distinct advantages when all other things are equal.

5. *Relevance.* Savvy businesses understand that their communities care most about the little things that only an insider would know. When you speak your community's language, you develop a bond that supports your business's ongoing relevance. And that language often includes the keyword phrases that optimize your online content for search.

This is all going to become even more interesting as a growing number of the members of the "Facebook generation" find their way into the workforce. You can expect business to become profoundly social, because that will be the expectation of your younger employees. Students in high school and college today have much different views of authority figures than their parents. While they respect authority figures and their positions, they also expect full access to them as well. This means that they will expect to have access to you as a business owner—just as your customers will.

One way to grant this access is to become personally involved with the implementation of your social marketing. You'll learn more about your customers, while also giving them the opportunity to learn more about you. This is what Tom Peters had in mind when he popularized the term Management By Walking Around (MBWA) in 1982 as the co-author of the groundbreaking business book *In Search of Excellence*. Thus, now you have social media to digitally facilitate walking around the communities your business serves, something your competitors may already be doing.

CONSUMERS HAVE A VOICE

The collective voice of consumers will continue to grow and shape the world of commerce. The challenge for businesses is to leverage its power by first engaging with it, and then facilitating the conversation to help the community do more of what it wants to do.

People want to be heard, and every business needs to provide a forum for that to happen. Many companies are using their Facebook page to accomplish this, which is smart, but only if the company monitors and manages the conversation. I happen to be a fan of Southwest Airlines. When they redesigned their rewards program, I went over to their Facebook page to do some research on whether to convert my old reward points or keep the free tickets from the earlier program. There was a lengthy string of hundreds of negative comments without a single response from Southwest. This was surprising because Southwest is a well-respected company that is known for their friendliness and personal engagement with customers. Unfortunately, the lack of response only served to fan the flames of customers who were looking for answers—and not finding them.

The worst thing a business or brand can do is fail to respond. If you are going to open up a Facebook page or accept comments on your blog, you have a responsibility to respond to your audience. That expectation doesn't seem to make sense to the same companies that will always answer the telephone if it rings. Today those calls may not be coming so much by the telephone as they are from the social networks. Is your business answering the call? It's an expectation that you must build into your standard business practices.

CUSTOMER SERVICE IS MOVING ONLINE

A growing number of consumers are becoming more comfortable openly expressing their true feelings online. While this scares the heck out of most businesses, it is something that we are all going to have to come to grips with. For that to happen, your business has to be willing to join the conversation and be prepared to make strong moves.

Business is no longer the monologue that it used to be when the message of the company was taken at face value. Now, it's a dialogue with increasingly vocal consumers. According to most research studies over the past several decades, approximately 70 to 80 percent of all consumers do not trust businesses in general, especially large corporations.

Your company should embrace this reality by using the social networks to proactively reach out to your customers. While taking this approach makes the company somewhat vulnerable, it is much less risky than creating perceived barriers when consumers expect transparency. Times are changing;

generally accepted practices are being redefined. Social media is making business in general more open by giving everyone equal access—as well as supporting the expectation that every customer will receive first-class service.

You can wait for this trend to become more mainstream, or you can take action now to lead your industry. The collective voice of consumers is growing more powerful every day—something that forward-thinking businesses know they can no longer ignore. One innovative approach is to give up control of your brand to consumers. Instead of trying to completely manage your brand, focus instead on encouraging community conversations that speak favorably about it.

One way to accomplish this is with digital social objects that effectively speak for the business across multiple social media channels, and that are strategically aligned with the business products and services that are also considered social objects in the real world.

SOCIAL OBJECTS

We discussed the concept of social graphs in the previous chapter—the means for digitally describing every individual and business on the respective social networks. Recall that these graphs are comprised of the information present in your account profiles, your connections, and your relationships with digital content in the form of photos, videos, audio, and text, otherwise known within the context of social media as social objects. That's the digital world, and Ford Motor Company is wisely using it to create digital social objects to encourage their customers to share their experiences about their automobiles with other like-minded Ford aficionados.

Now consider that you also have social objects in the real world—physical objects around which your customers engage. Ford Motor Company Chief Marketing Officer Jim

Farley notes that cars are social objects because people have a special relationship with their automobiles that make them much more than just modes of transportation. If you doubt this, consider that some people give their cars pet names to define their personal relationship with them.

Now consider what the social objects are in your business.

One example in mine might be an event at which I am speaking. Events are clearly interactive social experiences. A more tangible example is a good book. People like to share books by exchanging or recommending them to their friends (I would be delighted to have you do so with this one).

The challenge for online marketers is to create digital social objects and then strategically align them with the physical social objects of their business. Ford, for instance, scored a huge success when they made a $15,000 investment in a video that is approaching 50 million YouTube views. Contrast that with a Super Bowl commercial that costs millions of dollars, yet is forgotten days later. To watch the YouTube video, go to the Appendix for the link.

The Ford video is a digital object with a theoretically unlimited shelf life. It prompts both online and offline conversations that gets people into the Ford showrooms. The stories, photos, videos, and other digital objects that are shared on the social networks all create entry points to your business that can encourage those invaluable conversations that transform your actual products into social objects. This is an essential goal of your social media marketing.

SUSTAINING A BUSINESS IN THE TRUST ECONOMY

All things being equal, people will do business with the companies they know, like, and trust. In fact, even when all things are not equal, people will still choose to work with the businesses they trust. This is especially true in the economy we are now experiencing—one where minimizing risk is often more important to many people than maximizing gain.

GETTING CUSTOMERS TO KNOW YOUR BUSINESS

In order to get work these days, it is necessary to show that you want the work, you appreciate the work, and that you are easy to work with. You need to convey to customers that your business is friendlier, more accommodating, and more gracious than the others.

In the early days of modern marketing, advertising firms worked nearly exclusively for large consumer brands, promoting soaps and detergents, automobiles, cosmetics, and yes, cigarettes. All of these products had one thing in common: they were mass-produced. Thus, the role of advertising was to create a need for products that were already designed and, for the most part, produced as well. This strategy worked well during the post-World War II period when the economy was strong. It was the beginning of the age of consumerism for the growing middle class. People had discretionary income and were eager to exchange it for products that were advertised as new, better, and different.

In many ways, this was the heyday of traditional media, which consisted of radio, newspapers, magazines, and television. A small number of large organizations controlled the power of the media. Journalists and media personalities were even considered celebrities and, as a result, we learned to trust them. After all, you can't print what isn't true, right? As unbelievable as it sounds today, that was the mindset during the 1950s, 1960s, and maybe the 1970s. We believed what we read, heard on the radio, and viewed on television. Of course, there were standards and guidelines—or so we thought.

It turns out that not all advertising is truthful, and that not all products and services perform as promised. In fact, some of them had some serious side effects. This is when and where the lack of trust for larger organizations began to develop.

Nevertheless, media continued to proliferate because it was tightly controlled, and funded by organizations that desperately guarded that control to ensure their continued profitability. Phrases such as "buyer beware," "ripped off," and "Did you get it in writing?" became part of everyday conversations.

Given all of this history, is it any wonder that people today do not trust businesses? Times have certainly changed, haven't they? Now consumers expect to be served on time, receive a price that is no higher than your competitors, and get a full refund if they are not 100 percent satisfied.

Designing your business around social will soon be essential in markets where quality products and competitive pricing are expected. While consumers today are looking for reasons to like your company, that is not going to come from a traditional features and benefits message.

This is precisely why you should use social media to personalize your business. It's the ultimate differentiator—something that social media does exceptionally well. Is there an interesting backstory about how you got started or achieved your success? People are hungry to hear the personal stories and anecdotes that make companies unique. It makes you less of a "business" in their eyes, and more of a fellow human being.

You can study both traditional and new media to get ideas on what works. There is a reason the print publication *People* magazine continues to prosper in a declining industry; people are interested in people and their stories. You can share success stories about your employees, customers, or friends in the community. When you humanize your business in this way, you make it friendlier and more engaging.

LIKEABLE IS FOR BRANDS; FRIENDLY IS FOR BUSINESSES

Likeability in a business context used to be the stereotypical backslapping salesman or the "friend" who did you a favor in an effort to get what they wanted in return. We have all learned to recoil when these things happen. It's just a sign of the times; reciprocity is dead.

Customers don't want a favor; they simply want to get to know more about you as a person. The approach that Chrysler took—putting the CEO out front to meet and greet the brand's consumers—is literally what saved the company during the 1980s, and also resurrected Remington electric shavers during the late 1970s when its CEO did the same. But that is not enough to build trust today.

Now, everyone wants to get up close and personal, and they want to do it on their own terms, in an environment that gives them full access to ask questions, share with others, and speak their minds. This is the foundation of social media. Is your business ready to do this?

Just as Lee Iacocca saved Chrysler—and more recently, the late Steve Jobs saved Apple after previously being unceremoniously kicked out of the company he founded—you can and should take similar measures to transform your business. You have to get out there and be visible, authentic, human, genuine, honest—and even willing to be a little bit vulnerable.

There is no separation of personal and business anymore. Customers today want to know about your personal life because it helps them understand and relate to you, bringing you and your business ever closer to earning their vital trust. It works the same way in business as it does in politics and sports. Greater authenticity and personalization makes you friendlier, and that makes your business brand more likeable.

BUSINESS IN THE TRUST ECONOMY

Trust is the new celebrity power, and it's something that anyone can earn with the help of social media. You can literally be a celebrity in your industry or community based on the strength of your experience and expertise. Local celebrity power brings with it the ability to influence a specific community and move them to action. You develop this by consistently helping your community; and then, when the time is right, they will in turn be there to return the favor.

Social media is an organic process that works at your community's pace. However long it takes for them to trust you is how long it is going to take for it to work. Think of your community as your familiar tribe that will be there for you when the time is right to do business. Author and popular business blogger Seth Godin suggests that you "build your tribe" by focusing on helping those you can, while disregarding the others. You certainly won't be able to please everyone when you take a stand like this; however, you will better personalize your business for your tribe—your true fans—those that believe in you and your business.

Small businesses need to learn that differentiation is essential for them, specifically because they are not consumer brands. You are a business, and there is a world of difference. Brands are largely symbolic and general, whereas your business—and the good things it does for your community—is tangible and real.

To have more control over your social marketing, you have to give it up to the collective voice of the community that shapes public perception of your business. Use your social media to give your community something that gets them talking favorably about your business—then leverage its power.

When you do that, you respect the fact that nobody wants to be manipulated or pressured to buy. Instead, develop a community that wants to be connected with your business—a tribe of fans that share common interests. And what do fans do? They buy souvenirs.

We typically think of souvenirs as low-value, throwaway items. However, in our digital world—where so much is available for free—tangible items of all kinds are valued souvenirs of shared relationships. It's the reason why sports fans spend a fortune on memorabilia just to feel a stronger connection to a player or a team, and it's why some of your customers buy from you.

Many of your customers are your customers because they want to be connected with your business. They are your tribe, and their desire to be involved extends beyond the quality of your products and services. This likely includes the character of the people you employ and the company values that guide the service your business delivers.

In markets where quality is so high that consumers cannot easily discern significant differences, the differentiators are the subtle qualities associated with your business that you can amplify with solid social media networking and marketing. Focus on that to engage them and earn their trust and loyalty, and you will sustain your business.

Marketing today is driven by the customer. The old mindset dictated that you find customers for your products and services. The new one says: find or develop products and services for the customers whose trust you have earned. It's a fundamental shift that will grow and sustain your business in the trust economy.

Try This: Define Your Ideal Customer

The first step in any marketing plan is understanding your target audience—the customers that your business can ideally serve well.

Do you have a customer like Bob, one that really challenges your business—and makes it better?

Your ideal customers are those that reward you with repeat business, refer you, and especially challenge you to grow, thereby helping you serve all of your customers better.

- Who are a few of your clients or customers that fit some of these criteria and why? Write down your thoughts.

- Choose at least three qualities they all share.

- What is their number one challenge—the one that never seems to go away, and therefore needs fresh insights?

- How can you help them with this challenge? Write this out with as much detail as possible. Now you have the seeds of several articles for your blog or newsletter.

- Take these ideas and write three or four article headlines (using your keywords from Chapter 1) and a few sentences to capture the problems you are solving and how.

- Read the next chapter to learn more about how to get started (or better) with blogging.

CHAPTER 3

Every Business Is Now a
Media Company

The top blogs today are simply more relatable than traditional media,
which makes them cool—and that gets their content shared.

Consumers will always seek relevant news and information
to make better buying decisions. Before social media, their
primary sources for doing so were traditional media outlets
such as radio, television, newspapers, and, of course, word-of-
mouth. According to a study by Pew Research Center, the
Internet is now the leading source of information for consumers making buying decisions—ranking even higher than
the recommendations of their friends.

The idea that consumers trust the Internet more than their
friends may initially seem surprising. However, it's quite likely
that they're simply using the Internet to validate those recommendations. Of course, this spells opportunity for small
businesses that are ready to take the initiative with the considerable resources available to them to publish solutions online

that will attract the attention of consumers searching for them—especially those in their local communities.

Traditional media companies invest significantly in their media programming content to build their audience. Their reward is what follows—the opportunity to generate revenue with advertising placements. As a media savvy small business, you have to focus on serving up valuable programming, too—information that will educate your customers, thereby making them better buyers. Your reward is earning their permission to market and sell your products and services. While there are responsibilities associated with being a media company—such as consistently producing great content—the business benefits greatly outweigh the efforts you'll make.

It is safe to say that small businesses will never experience a marketing opportunity like this again. To have the freedom of controlling your own media is something you should not take lightly, because it gives you the power to compete with companies that may have far greater resources. No longer is the business with the splashiest advertising the likely choice for buyers. Social media instead favors those who are willing to work to help their customers by giving them the information they need in the form of valuable content.

Content is still and will always be king, which means that content marketing is uniquely suited to helping businesses like yours attract new customers.

MARKETERS ARE NOW TEACHERS

Successful marketing is a practice of educating buyers before, during, and after the sale. Serving as a resource and guide for your customers is a sure way to earn their trust. That is the essence of content marketing—teaching your customers what they need to know to do more of what they want to do. For instance, let's say you are selling lawn mowers. You can teach customers how the machines operate, but how do you get them into the door to take that action? You may consider using your content marketing to promote the benefits of a healthy lawn so they will want to buy a lawn mower in the first place.

This concept carries over into countless industries, products, and services. If you are buying running shoes, you will value the opinions of experienced runners. If you are buying live plants for your garden, you want to buy them from someone who has used them and experienced first-hand how they respond to varying environmental conditions. And if you are going into surgery, you definitely want a doctor with years of experience on his or her side. This should excite small businesses who may be overwhelmed by online marketing, yet have the necessary practical experience to succeed with it.

There is no substitute for experience when helping customers, especially when they do not even know what questions they should be asking to make good decisions. One reason is that much of what they need to know has traditionally been guarded by businesses to protect their market position and margins. However, this is increasingly difficult for companies to pull off as consumers are becoming more discerning and better educated. Leading businesses have recognized this reality and are pulling back the curtain to show them what others are not willing to share. Buyers appreciate that, value it, and will remember it when it comes to making their next purchase.

One of the best ways to find out how to help your buyers is already online. Their questions are buried within the comments found on industry blogs, Amazon ratings, and YouTube. When you begin to see the same questions again and again, you know you've found an opportunity. In fact, that is precisely how I came to write this book. The small businesses with whom I interact every day often ask me for a book on social marketing that is written specifically for them—by someone that has walked in their shoes, understands their challenges and opportunities, and speaks their language.

You probably remember your favorite teacher in elementary or high school. Chances are they were the one with an ability to relate well to the students. That is what made them popular and cool. You can try to be cool, as many marketers do, or you can just be relatable and let cool be a by-product. That's one of the secrets of being a successful content marketing teacher—develop the skill of relating to your community and everything else will take care of itself, including customers asking to do business with you.

BUILDING THE CLASSROOM

Imagine a business environment where the solution to every problem is immediately available. This might sound far-fetched, but it is not fantasy. The tools and methods for making this happen are here, right now. And smart businesses are consistently using them to provide timely and relevant solutions to the most pressing needs of their customers.

Digital communication technologies are becoming increasingly uncomplicated, making it possible—even easy—for small businesses to use them to build their own business media channel. The foundation of this channel is a first-class blog that businesses can use to actively address the ongoing needs of their defined customers.

Think about it from the perspective of being a consumer yourself: Wouldn't you like to have easy access to fresh updates on the products and services you regularly use? Your customers are no different. They have been conditioned to expect answers whenever they need them, and your business has a responsibility to provide this service for them.

Perhaps you're currently communicating with your customers through your e-mail newsletter—and you should continue to do this. Yet, we all know that despite our best efforts our newsletters may not hit the mark when they are initially received, with the information then being deleted and lost forever—and that is if they manage to get through the spam filters.

A blog that serves up time-tested, evergreen content is a viable alternative. It is an invaluable content marketing asset whose value builds and grows over time, thereby serving as an attraction vehicle for teaching new customers what they want to learn, while also helping them to get to know your company.

Today's top business blogs are some of the most valued sources of fresh and relevant news and useful information. Your content marketing blog is your classroom. As such, you can use it to teach what you know to attract customers that have been searching the web for a company just like yours.

EVERGREEN CONTENT CURRICULUM

Content marketing has been around since before the Internet in other formats. My use of it for launching my small business in the 1980s is just one example. Did you also know that soap operas were developed as the content to attract an audience to sell detergent and other soaps during television commercials? This is how they came to be known as "soap operas." The evolution of the Internet—along with the capability of blogging—now empowers businesses like yours and mine that are ready to attract our own audience with content marketing.

There were few rules in the early days of blogging—and not many more today—except for some oversight by the FTC with respect to full disclosure on such matters as endorsements. However, as blogging matures and search engines continue to improve how they do their job, there are some emerging trends you should know about.

The most notable of these is greater professionalism that is taking content marketing to another level, with the better bloggers borrowing best practices from traditional media sources. In fact, as a result of their focus on niche communities, the top blogs today are often more respected than the traditional media sources they are copying. Why? They are simply more relatable; this makes them cool, and that compels more people to share their content on the social networks.

If you want your blog to gain enough respect to earn an audience, you'll need to start thinking like a media company. Following are a few simple guidelines to help you shape your blog's structure and content to make it your content marketing hub.

Organize Your Information

Early blogs used archives and categories to organize information; however, this is becoming somewhat obsolete. Just as your business processes must adapt to changing conditions, so too have the methods for successfully blogging. Your first job is to guide your visitor. Consider adding a "start here" tab and then organizing your best articles into a series of mini-classes or subject matter tutorials.

Keep Your Information Up-to-Date

Google wants what people want: the most up-to-date information they can find on a particular subject. By consistently publishing fresh content to your blog, you are serving both your customers and the search engines that will help you find new customers.

Publish Relevant Information

The more you blog, the more you will learn how to help your customers, particularly if you are paying attention to comments and what earns greater sharing with their social networks. You will begin to realize after a few years of blogging that the most relevant issues change slowly, if at all. For example, I recently read a business publication that interviewed several leading snow plowing contractors about the future of their businesses. All of their comments circled back to one challenge nearly every business shares: getting new customers and making the current ones happy while still turning a profit.

Thus, your organized, up-to-date, and relevant information should ideally be the kind of enduring evergreen content that will serve your customers today and tomorrow. You can organize this information into tutorials, a series of eBooks, online classes, instructional case studies, and more. The goal is to be what you would want to find if you were one of your customers (or Google helping them)—the source for the best, most relevant, and organized information for a particular problem or category of problems.

YOUR COLLECTIVE BUSINESS CHANNEL

In addition to the major social media networks such as Facebook, LinkedIn, Twitter, and now Google+, there are other networks such as Foursquare and Pinterest that are also earning their rightful place as sources of online traffic. The combined mix of these—along with your blogs, websites, and e-mail newsletters—are what we will collectively call your business channel. Your business needs to make some decisions with respect to the respective elements that comprise this channel, so that you can then determine how to best accomplish your business objectives.

In order to persuade your audience to consistently engage with your social media channel, you have to provide programming that delivers value. This could come in the form of solutions to common problems or ideas that are relevant to their lives. Obviously, this programming should be related in some way to the products and services that your business offers. For example, I had learned from my speaking engagements that many businesses are challenged with deciding if they should use social media for their business or personally. So, I wrote a blog post on this and it earned a lot of traffic, which told me it was on target. As a result, I wrote a similar post about a year later from a new perspective and it earned even more traffic.

To get ideas on what works, study both traditional and new media. One approach—as we've discussed previously—is to share success stories about your employees, customers, or friends in the community. Stories that illustrate how your business achieved a successful outcome for one of your customers are especially valuable. This will help your visitors to your site recognize their circumstances within those situations, and thereby envision how your business could help them.

Whatever social networks you favor—be it Facebook, Twitter, YouTube, or any of the others—your approach is essentially the same. You want to share content across multiple networks to attract and hold your audience's attention so that you can occasionally make business offers. It's a process of earning attention, then familiarity, and finally, trust.

THINKING LIKE A MEDIA COMPANY

One of the reasons your social media marketing may not be as effective as you'd like is that it works much like a traditional medium with which you probably have little or no experience—television. But chances are that you're a television viewer and consumer yourself. So you have a general idea about what people—especially your customers and their influencers in your local community—will tune into.

To use social media well, you have to think like a media company—such as NBC, ESPN, or HBO. All of these companies manage multiple networks or channels that collectively represent one business brand. Once you develop that media company mindset, you will be better equipped to build a more effective social media business presence—one you can fine-tune as you acquire more experience.

PROVIDE VALUABLE PROGRAMMING

It takes work to plan good programming, and it takes even more work to create and produce it. This is one reason why it is more popular to share social content than create it, and why you can quickly become a leader in your community and industry if you are willing to be a content creator.

Businesses should have a good idea how to attract and retain customers; otherwise, they wouldn't be in business. One of the challenges is to discern the one, two, or three most important things about your business that have helped get you to this level, and then breathe those qualities into your social media.

The following are some of the essential criteria to consider when designing your programming.

- *What is your core business message?* What do you want to be known for? For example, Domino's Pizza formerly promised, "Your pizza will arrive within 30 minutes or it's free."

- *What is the best medium for delivering it?* Is the written word better than audio or video? Video is highly effective, but it's not always ideal. For instance, it may be a problem in office environments.

- *What are your best channels?* Is Facebook better than LinkedIn for your business? Most businesses should consider using both, for reasons discussed in Chapter 1.

- *What secondary channels will prove useful?* For video and photos, platforms such as YouTube, Facebook, and now Pinterest seem essential.

- *What will be your sources of programming ideas?* In addition to your own business, you can discover relevant ideas from industry blogs using sites such as Alltop.com and Technorati.com.

- *Who will be the star or stars of your show?* Will you be sharing the responsibilities with other team members? Will you accept guest articles?

- *How frequently will you publish?* This can vary. More important than frequency is consistency. Nothing turns away an audience more quickly than a blog or Facebook page that has apparently been abandoned.

- *What formats or structure will you use?* Among other options, you can consider doing a series of programs on a particular topic or stand-alone programs to keep things simple.

Here are seven media formats you can use to build your programming.

1. The how-to
2. Expert viewpoints or perspectives
3. Interviews
4. Product or service reviews
5. Trends and best practices
6. Helpful tools, tips, and techniques
7. Business promotions

While all of this may seem complicated, you can learn it fairly easily—if you simply get in the game. In fact, that is the only way to learn. There isn't a single person who has mastered this any other way.

ENGAGE THE COMMUNITY

Consumers today are looking for reasons to like your company and that is readily accomplished if you use social marketing to personalize your business. This means you will need to seed your business channel with honest and authentic stories, which is easier than you may think.

One approach to consider is creating a reality show. For example, a restaurant business can take their audience back into the kitchen to showcase some of the details they do not usually get to see, but that obviously contribute significantly to the overall dining experience. Isn't this why people tune into The Food Network?

You can create your reality show on your own television station—what you know as YouTube. Then share it on Facebook, your company blog, and all of the other channels you have established. Use your uniqueness to differentiate your business by taking advantage of what each specific network does best with the respective types of media. By all means, test and experiment to find out what works best for connecting with your community.

What makes social media uniquely different from most other forms of media is that it is interactive. It combines traditional broadcasting, reality television, and word-of-mouth all rolled into one. And as we all know, word-of-mouth is one of the most powerful means for keeping your sales pipeline full.

You'll have a difficult time achieving this, however, if you do not engage your audience and respond to their inquiries. Business is no longer on a standard clock or calendar. It's now running 24/7 and it's global. While most consumers do not expect you to respond 24/7, they do expect reasonable timeliness. I know you may be thinking these are unrealistic expectations, but it's the collective community that makes the rules. If you do the best you can, your customers will certainly notice and appreciate that effort.

HOW BLOGGING MAKES YOUR BUSINESS BETTER

Most people tend to think of blogging as writing. But after nearly seven years of blogging consistently, I have come to realize the interaction and engagement associated with it makes blogging much more than that.

The digital blogging platform works much like face-to-face situations in which you are engaged with your customers. There is a message, an audience, and most importantly, there is a relationship with that audience.

If getting in front of your customers makes you a better marketing, sales, or customer service professional, then regular blogging will accelerate your progress, too—with the difference being it's all done virtually. Here's how it works: every experience we have is processed in our minds. So, regardless of whether the experience is digital or face-to-face, it is still real as far as the mind is concerned. It's a lot like what happens when you go to the movies; you have learned to suspend your disbelief, thereby enabling you to experience the film as if it were real.

You are also able to suspend your disbelief when you blog. This helps make the virtual platform experience real, thereby allowing you to gain invaluable experience in a short period of time. As a result, you discover new and innovative ways to help your customers. For instance, you can use a negative customer experience as a case study to help not just one particular customer, but your entire community. Fixing mistakes in this way is a very humanizing and an engaging use of your blog.

So, why are so few businesses actively blogging? It's likely because they do not understand how it can make their business better. Here are three ways it can.

1. *Enhance Your Customer Service.*

   When you blog regularly, you learn more about your customers. You get better at discovering their most relevant needs and developing solutions to their problems. It may not be possible to physically be with your customers every day, but you can use your blog to virtually connect with them as often as you wish.

2. *Showcase Your Expertise.*

   A well-designed blog focuses on solving the specific problems of a defined group. In this respect, every blog post is a piece of living and breathing content that validates your expertise. When you augment that content with images, audio, and video it tells a story that makes your expertise come alive.

3. *Product and Service Innovation.*

   When you skillfully encourage conversations with your audience, you develop relationships and build trust. The more you practice achieving that engagement, the more proficient you will get at growing your blog community. Start by making visitors feel welcome by thoughtfully responding to each and every comment.

HOW TO START BLOGGING

Despite the fact that there are millions of blogs on the web, the percentage of active *small business bloggers* in any mainstream industry besides technology is typically below 20 percent, and probably closer to 10 percent or less. There indeed are some challenges associated with the practice of blogging; however, there are also solutions for working around them, and rewards associated with making it well worth the effort.

Common Blogging Challenges

Let's take a look at some of the common challenges, some suggested solutions for overcoming them, and then a step-by-step process for how to start a blog. While the percentage of bloggers is small, it is not for lack of desire. What we hear most often is that "I know I should be doing this, but . . . (insert excuse here)."

So, let's address the top challenges that are holding many people back. Prioritized according to frequency, they are:

1. I don't have enough time.
2. I'm not a very good writer.
3. What should I blog about?
4. How often should I blog?
5. How do I start a blog?

Some solutions can solve several challenges at once. For example, if you are not a talented writer you can post a short video or an image with a compelling caption to solve the challenges of time and writing skill.

Regarding the question of how often one should blog, it really comes down to a straightforward question: How good do you want to be?

Whether your blog content is primarily written, an audio podcast, or video, it will start with writing, which is like a muscle that you have to use to make it stronger. Every writer will tell you this, including luminaries such as Stephen King, who wrote an outstanding book on the craft, *On Writing*. It's an educational and entertaining account of Stephen King's early efforts to break into the business, and his journey to overcome challenges to be the highly respected author he is today.

What to blog about is not only a challenge for new bloggers, but also those of us that have been doing this for years. You will discover most people are hungry for tips and advice, insights on future trends, and step-by-step methods for getting things done. For example, if you Google "LinkedIn" it will suggest "tips" as the most searched term associated with that keyword. Thus, whenever I write about LinkedIn, I frame my blog posts as tips because that is what people are evidently most interested in learning about. (See Figures 3.1 and 3.2.)

Two things to know about blogging: it takes patience, and struggle is an essential component of the content-creation process. It takes time to build an audience; yet that effort ultimately results in creating the quality of work necessary for growing it. The process can be compared to growing world-class winemaking grapes. The harder the vine works to produce the few clusters of grapes from the gravelly soil, the more intense the fruit—thereby producing magical wines that thrill the senses.

Think of your blog as sort of a laboratory or proving ground. It's a great place to try out new ideas. It doesn't matter whether you have an audience in the early stages. In fact,

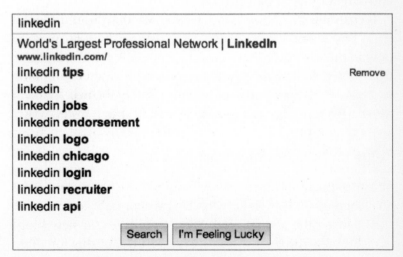

Figure 3.1   Google search for LinkedIn

Figure 3.2   Google search results for LinkedIn tips showing original article by author, with Google Authorship attribution

every blog has one very important audience member: Google. Work hard for Google by creating quality content that it can send to those searching for it, and it will reward your blog with higher search rankings.

Remember that people are seeking solutions to their problems. This is one reason I like to say that small companies are now in the *answers business*. (See the Appendix for more on this from an article with an informative video.) If you use your blog to create and share answers to common problems, you will never have to worry about ranking well in search results again.

Steps for Successfully Starting a Blog

Step One: Define the community. You need to clearly define your readers. Have a mental picture of who they are, where they are located, what they want to know, and how they will most likely prefer to consume your content (written, video, audio, etc.).

Step Two: Know why you are blogging. What action do you want your readers to take? Do you want them to subscribe to your blog, leave a comment, share it with their Facebook friends, or sign up for your newsletter? Whatever your primary purpose, be sure to include the appropriate call-to-action near the close of each post or article.

Step Three: Determine what you most want to write about. Blogging is a lot like exercise: you have to choose something you enjoy if you are going to do it consistently. So, choose subject matter that interests both you and your target audience.

Step Four: Determine what is not being done that is of value to your community. You can address underserved needs in your markets. Start by subscribing to other blogs and read the comments to learn what the needs are that other businesses either cannot or will not tackle.

Step Five: Choose a descriptive title and subtitle for your blog. Your blog should instantly communicate a specific purpose for your ideal audience. A memorable title with a descriptive subtitle is always best, such as Search Engine Land: News About Search Engines and Search Marketing (SearchEngineLand.com). The focus of this popular blog is clear and the main title is sufficiently memorable.

Step Six: Write a compelling bio that describes your expertise and personality, or that of the business. A few sentences that capture your personality, key credentials, and special skills are essential.

Step Seven: Choose a blog platform that allows you to own your content. While there are other blogging platforms such as Blogger, Typepad, and Tumblr, a self-hosted Wordpress blog is becoming nearly universal for those serious about blogging for practical business results.

Step Eight: Start blogging. While it's easy to start blogging, it's not quite as easy to keep up with it, especially when you're trying to determine what to write about. Look for inspiration from helping just one person and you will soon discover you have done so for others as well.

Step Nine: Blog consistently and never stop learning. The most important time to stay with your blogging is when you least want to. That's when you will make the breakthroughs that will carry you to the next level—where it will then get easier.

WEBSITE ARCHITECTURE FOR YOUR CONTENT

Many consumers are on a short timetable and are mostly concerned about product and service details because they are ready to buy. If this describes your typical buyer, then the home page of your website should be laser-focused on the details associated with your product offerings. For most businesses it's necessary to do the work of attracting new buyers to your website, and then educating them when they get there by making the blog integral to the home page.

Remember that search drives the web, and that is why Google loves blogs that consistently serve up fresh and useful content. When your blog is primary to the home page of your website, it sends a signal to Google that the page is educational as well as commercial. This enhances the potential search ranking of your website by introducing relevant content.

One of the more promising site design options these days is a hybrid site that combines the best qualities of a blog and traditional website. One approach to this is having your primary products and services front and center above the fold (top of the page) on your site's home page—with just the most recent blog posts below the fold (and the full blog on a secondary page). This effectively monetizes your site by keeping your commerce primary, while also taking advantage of the SEO benefits of combining fresh blog content on that same page.

Since your complete blog will be sitting on the secondary navigation of your website, the hybrid approach maximizes the most valuable real estate of your website. For clarity, host the most recent blog content on the yoursite.com home page, with the complete blog on yoursite.com/blog.

THE RESPONSIBILITIES OF A MEDIA COMPANY

Radio personalities know to avoid "dead air"—the uncomfortable silence associated with an interruption in the broadcasted audio—at all costs. The likelihood of listeners tuning out increases with every passing second. In the award-winning film *The Social Network*, based upon the early days of Facebook, there is an important and emphatic statement made by Facebook founder Mark Zuckerberg: "We don't go down—ever!"

That's the mindset your company should bring to your social networking. Clearly, you cannot always be on Facebook; however, you must honor certain programming times in the same way that a traditional media channel would. In other words, whenever possible you have to set notifications using apps such as Nimble.com to monitor your channels, and using publishing tools such as Hootsuite.com and Bufferapp .com to schedule content for future delivery, and otherwise be available to respond to your community.

Being available requires that you seek to avoid the common "tweet and run" practice. We all know that many tweets and other social media posts are automated, and you can certainly take that approach. However, it is wise to pick periodic times during the day to regularly be available.

Your business should also address any open issues that could otherwise incur negative comments. For instance, I'm waiting right now for a response regarding an iPad app that is buggy and needs some fixes. Since the developer has tweeted they are working on it, they have fulfilled their duty as a media company for the time being.

When you fail to respond—even just to let customers know that you are "working on it"—you lose the confidence that may have taken months or even years to earn. Attention is something that is going to be harder to come by as more people use social media more effectively. This is why you need to respond when you have your community's attention, because there are lots of folks, such as your competitors, who may be watching to see if you do exactly that.

Of course, you will occasionally receive negative responses on the networks that comprise your collective business channel; this is something that is nearly unavoidable. However, a skillful response can turn a complaint into a new fan. It happens all the time. The most crucial thing is to acknowledge that you've received the complaint; then offer a solution or a promise to circle back with a progress report. Whatever you do, be friendly and do not make excuses. That alone will earn the respect of the majority.

Ideally, you will want to have a community manager, one who leads your efforts. Larger organizations have multiple managers to provide greater coverage. But even this can lead to challenges, since they will all manage problems differently without clear guidelines. However it is accomplished, the real shift for businesses comes from the mindset of a community of people, rather than a market of customers. This is what we'll cover in the next chapter.

Try This: Build Your Business Channel

Imagine you have unlimited funds to hire a media company to produce all of your content (this takes the burden of work out of the equation).

What would you like your media company to create for your business that will dazzle your customers and attract more of them?

- Are you thinking a TV or radio program, or possibly a digital magazine?

- Brainstorm with your team about what will work best for your audience before implementing the practices you learned in this chapter.

- Start designing and prioritizing the media mix to build your business channel. TV is video. Radio is podcasting. And a blog is a digital magazine.

- Read Chapter 4 to learn more about building your business channel. If you prefer to learn with video, there are thousands of step-by-step video tutorials on virtually every aspect of social media at Grovo.com.

PART TWO

Engagement: Social Networking and Marketing

CHAPTER 4

Communities Are the New Markets

People live and work in communities, not markets. The challenge for any business is to simply get out into the community and make friends.

When I was earning my MBA in the early 1980s, our marketing studies naturally involved the study of markets. We learned strategies that major brands of the time used to "attack" markets to gain market share that contributed to the growth of the enterprise. A successful attack usually meant that competitors were harmed, in the sense that market share was taken away from them. We learned tactics such as market segmentation, where, if a market was large, you could consider dividing it to conquer a particular portion, such as an age or lifestyle demographic.

The explicit goal was to carve out a segment whose needs could be better served with products designed specifically for them. A classic example at that time was the rivalry between Coke and Pepsi. Pepsi was favored by younger and more hip buyers, so who better to help them target that demographic than the larger-than-life pop icon Michael Jackson?

What's interesting is that much of the marketing practices were borrowed—from the strategies to the language used for dominating markets—from one familiar model: the military. In fact, in a popular film of that era, *Wall Street*, there is a scene where protagonist Gordon Gecko recommends to his protégé Bud Fox that he read *The Art of War*, the ancient military treatise attributed to Sun Tzu, a ranking Chinese military general from the second century BC.

Corporate enterprises typically approached markets by conducting extensive research to determine the innovations that could lead them to increased market share. This was an intensive and time-consuming effort that churned out massive amounts of data for analysis. They then used it to design prototypes and trials that generated still more data. After a period of time it was necessary to decide how to proceed—a decision that was always made at the executive level, and based upon the data, of course.

Decisions on whether to proceed with new product ideas were often shuttled back and forth between a number of groups, including market research, research and development, business development, and new product development. These distinct departments or divisions may consist of dozens to hundreds of employees. As you can imagine, some ideas could be in the system for years. And to be honest, most were ultimately eliminated for one common reason: the market opportunity had passed.

That traditional top-down, bureaucratic approach to business was a primary reason that corporations had to endure years of painful downsizing. It should not come as a surprise to many that during the years of corporate layoffs, it was those research and business development departments—the parts with little or no customer contact—that were hit the hardest.

As for those of us working directly with customers in marketing and sales, our jobs were spared. Thankfully, most businesses today understand that this is where business development starts: with customers, not markets. Markets are an artificial construct that is of limited use in a practical business model, especially for mainstream small businesses.

Customers live in communities, not markets. The focus of every business should be getting to know the people in the communities they serve so that they can serve them even better. There is nothing to segment, divide, or conquer—just people to get to know so that the business can learn how to help them improve their quality of life.

THE COMMUNITY ECOSYSTEM

Communities are indeed the new markets. People live and work in communities and many of them are your friends. Thus, the challenge for any business is to simply get out there and make friends. Get to know people. Understand them, and help them understand your business and its mission. This means being visible and engaged, which is a new approach that befuddles some businesses that still cling to the bureaucratic model.

Learning to think in terms of communities instead of markets requires that you embrace the concept of the social community as an ecosystem—a group of people who are in some way connected to and dependent upon everyone else. For the community to prosper, everyone within it has to get what they want—but not at the expense of others. Thus, the more a business uses its expertise and experience to solve common problems—even though they may not seem to directly serve your business mission—it increases the likelihood that other community members will support the business.

Business today is not about winning and losing; it's about everybody winning. Strategic social media marketing teaches us a great deal about the community ecosystem. We know that it's only possible to achieve a strong online presence when the community has your back, and that happens when you are freely contributing value—giving away lots of useful content, and doing it again and again until you feel like you are giving away too much.

Then one day it starts to come back. A few good things happen, then a few more, and then suddenly your business is growing more quickly than you could have imagined. It's a courtship with the community that honors everyone's needs, and it all extends outward to other communities.

Since we all live on one planet, we are by definition all part of the same community; the smaller communities intersect and overlap to connect everyone with everyone else. It may take some time for people around the globe to embrace this concept; however it's gaining traction, and little by little, it is changing the socio-economic practices around the world. The social web is more than a metaphor for how this works; it is the mechanism, too.

WHEN THE BUSINESS IS THE COMMUNITY

If you have ever worked in a company town, you understand that the community prospers and everyone is happy when the company is doing well. That was my experience while living in the small town of Bartlesville, Oklahoma, which at the time was the world headquarters for Phillips Petroleum Company (Phillips 66). The company town model has merit for communities of all sizes, including larger cities, because it creates greater awareness of the interdependencies between businesses and the community.

There is an interesting case study of this developing in Las Vegas. Online retailer Zappos is moving their operations from suburban Henderson, NV, to the old Las Vegas City Hall, a part of the city that has mostly been forgotten about, and is certainly not on the radar of most visitors to this city. But Zappos CEO Tony Hsieh has a vision of transforming downtown Las Vegas to create "the most community-focused large city in the world, in the place you probably least expect to see it."

Hsieh describes his remake for old Las Vegas as a win-win for Zappos, for local businesses, and for the city. The vision is analogous to how social media works to increase the likelihood of serendipitous happenings. In many ways, it is a practical application of how the intersection of real-life social connections can create new relationships, opportunities, and the inspiration for active involvement in a community.

Needless to say, there many supporters watching Zappos's every move and applauding their efforts to create an interactive, cohesive, and therefore sustainable community ecosystem.

THE SOCIAL BUSINESS MODEL

The new social business model is neither purely capitalist nor social. Rather, it's a hybrid that balances the community's needs. The term *social business* has traditionally been used to describe a business that exists predominantly to serve a social cause. Today its use and meaning is becoming much more broadly applied in the same way that social marketing is.

Every community has unmet or ongoing needs that are becoming the responsibility not just of the citizens, but also the businesses that the community supports. The old capitalistic model was one in which businesses functioned exclusively to make a profit, and from that they could choose to support community needs or not. These days, however, innovative approaches to business are changing everything.

SOCIAL ENTREPRENEURSHIP

If your business model is all business, then you may need to augment it to work more effectively in a world that is becoming profoundly social. Social entrepreneurship is now one of the hottest areas of study in top business schools such as Yale, Duke, USC—and my alma mater, Miami University in Oxford, OH.

One of the most notable examples of social entrepreneurship is TOMS Shoes. They are a for-profit company based in Santa Monica, CA, that donates one pair of shoes to underprivileged children in South America and other parts of the world for every pair that it sells. They call this their "one for one" interpretation of the social entrepreneurship business model. TOMS has not only given away millions of pairs of shoes since 2007, they also have attracted top talent and designs from the likes of Ralph Lauren. The TOMS model is intentionally quite simple, and that's a key reason it works.

Social entrepreneurship augments the traditional business profit motive by linking it with social or community causes. The two are combined into one business model that is highly relevant in our current business environment. We live in a global economy. All of these communities touch each other in some way—which means that we have to solve them at home first. Your customers understand this, so you need to, as well.

The way out of this broken economy is for all of us to realize that we have to work together. We must acknowledge that if you have a problem, then I have a problem. And social networks are communicating that message at lightning speed. As a business owner, when the communities you serve prosper, it creates abundance that can be shared with your business. Businesses are also in a position to use their knowledge and experience—plus this revolutionary marketing platform known as social networking—to help make that happen.

Of course, notable brands—such as Ben and Jerry's Ice Cream and outdoor gear and apparel company Patagonia—have incorporated philanthropy into their business model for decades. Many small businesses, such as my own landscape company, have also built their reputation as local community supporters. The difference is that it matters more today, and for a number of reasons.

In the kind of restrictive economy we're experiencing, it's simply not socially acceptable to make excessive profits without giving back to the community in some way. However, if a company can incorporate community sharing and giving into their approach, the business becomes more attractive to consumers who will respect and honor their community contributions—and likely buy from them as a result. The trick is to bake this into the business design instead of just making it an afterthought. This transparency naturally earns the trust of the community—and their support, too.

THE CURE STARTS NOW

More businesses are partnering with other organizations in their community as they are discovering the ways in which it enables them to better accomplish their respective goals. An interesting example of this came to my attention a couple of years ago while traveling through Cincinnati, OH. I noticed a billboard off the highway with the curious words: "scan. lick. cure." (See Figure 4.1.)

Figure 4.1   Cones for the Cure billboard with QR code

When I arrived at my hotel, my Google search for "scan, lick, and cure" returned a Facebook page that used a QR code as the profile photo. (More on QR codes in Chapter 7.) A quick scan of the code with my iPhone led me to the Cones for the Cure website, which provided an explanation for this joint effort between Cincinnati-based Graeter's Ice Cream with The Cure Starts Now Foundation.

In a nutshell: Graeter's created a special flavor of ice cream to benefit The Cure Starts Now, a nonprofit foundation launched in 2007 to honor Elena, the six-year-old daughter of customers Keith and Brooke Desserich, who died of brain cancer. From the Cones for the Cure landing page you enter your contact information to receive a coupon for a free scoop of Elena Blueberry Pie ice cream—and the opportunity to make a contribution to the foundation.

The billboard campaign was so successful that, in addition to the funds raised from individuals, Graeter's enjoyed increased revenue that covered their contributions. Additionally, the effort attracted other community businesses that wanted to partner with The Cure Starts Now to participate in future campaigns—and some of them now do. This is exactly what happened when TOMS Shoes began to find their way; others began reaching out to help.

The premise is quite simple: both nonprofits and for-profit businesses share the same demographic, so it was a partnership that was practically guaranteed to succeed—and it did. The challenge for businesses, therefore, is to change their thinking from a traditional model to a more socially-minded one.

For an excellent resource on business models, you may wish to consider investigating the book *Business Model Generation* by Alexander Osterwalder and Yves Pigneur (John Wiley & Sons, 2010). This comprehensive book provides a structure to help you examine your model with fresh eyes—and in an interactive team setting.

EACH SOCIAL CHANNEL IS A DISTINCT COMMUNITY

There are as many ways to use the social networks as there are businesses. And while you can learn a lot by studying other companies, you'll ultimately have to make decisions as to what works best to accomplish your business objectives. Build your presence by implementing the information presented here, then periodically assess your results to reallocate your resources accordingly. To be clear: there is no one right way to do this. And if anyone tries to tell you there is, run like crazy in the opposite direction.

In contrast to most forms of traditional marketing, one of the strengths of social media marketing is its capabilities for customizing your message for a specific community. Unfortunately, too many businesses tend to ignore the culture of their communities and simply blast a promotional message across all of their channels. Then they wonder why they aren't getting results.

As a professional speaker who works predominantly with mainstream small business groups and the organizations that support them, I have to consider the subtle differences and distinctions every time I get in front of these groups, even if I have previously spoken to that audience. Factors such as general business conditions, the time of year, and even the location will all dictate small adjustments in my approach. You will want to take a similar approach with each of your social media communities.

In the early days of social media, the objective seemed to be accumulating a progressively longer list of friends or followers. While there is still some value to this tactic, it's far wiser to make full use of each network's features to subdivide your communities further to better focus your communications. Your behavior on Facebook, for example, will understandably differ from that on the other social networks. Getting that right is priority number one. You can then take that to the next level by using whatever means are available—including lists, groups, and tags—to organize your friends and followers.

In the previous chapter we discussed that your evergreen content should be organized, up-to-date, and relevant to the community you are serving. Logically, the same applies to the respective social networks where you are sharing that information or having conversations associated with it. The better you organize your communities, the easier it is to be relevant. Just as a keynote presentation is designed to be general in order to be relevant to a large group, more intimate gatherings call for more personalized interactions.

LITTLE THINGS OFTEN MATTER THE MOST

Ask yourself: What are the especially important nuances associated with each respective channel that affect how and what to share? For instance, you would probably agree that Facebook is for showing off. So, if you want to make new friends and engage well with your current ones, you should avoid throwing cold water on anyone's party. In other words, the truth doesn't always play so well on Facebook—and the other networks as well, to some extent. That may sound inauthentic, but the fact is that it works the same way in real life. You simply cannot share everything that's on your mind without filtering a little out of respect for the community culture and other people's feelings.

If we revisit our overall objective of building the best business channel possible, you realize that it is vital to take a selective approach that maximizes the value each network has to offer. Remember that you are marketing—slowly building and enhancing your business's reputation. It's very easy to lose yourself in the context of the social interactions and forget that. Just be aware of checking your behavior every now and then in accordance with what plays well with a particular group. A good rule to follow is: When in doubt, leave it out.

The following are the major social media networks that every business should consider using. There are very specific reasons each one is included. There are clearly others, including the many sites for hosting and sharing video, audio, and photos. And there are certain businesses that may wish to devote even more attention to the alternatives than to these. However, most small businesses will find the following networks and associated best practices will provide a viable foundation for developing your social media communities well.

A brief description of the most salient aspects of each network along with key best practices follows. Please understand this is not intended to be a comprehensive treatment. Complete books have been written to cover all the details involved in getting the most from these channels, with many focused exclusively on just one. Yet one problem, as you might imagine, is that they are often out of date by the time they are published. Use these sources as you will, but be sure to subscribe to the respective Facebook, LinkedIn, Twitter, and Google+ blogs to keep current on how the platforms are operating. (Go to the Appendix for links.)

Every one of these networks maintains at least one blog that publishes timely updates to help you stay on top of your game. You will find that they do not publish all that frequently; however, when they do, they present the information in a user-friendly manner suitable for almost anyone.

FACEBOOK

The culture of Facebook favors informal interaction among friends. How this works for you personally is determined by your definition of friends, and the privacy settings that you choose. While a conservative approach limits your community, it also leads to higher quality interactions—something that you can also accomplish by organizing your friends with lists.

Be advised that Facebook plays for keeps when it comes to their terms of service. Therefore, establishing multiple accounts or engaging in other abuses can lead to termination of your account without notice.

Best Practices

- Facebook is a highly social community with an emphasis on sharing. You will get the most out of Facebook by freely sharing interesting or useful information.

- Facebook is a community that is largely invisible to Google. That's why you need a dual social marketing strategy that accommodates both Facebook and at least one of the other major networks indexed by Google.

- Facebook is a filtered experience. This means that what appears in your newsfeed is adjusted according to social signals, which are interactions such as sharing, comments, and likes. For this reason, you may wish to experiment with Facebook ads and promoted posts. They are still economical, although results vary significantly. (Read more about Facebook in Chapter 1.)

- Think of your Facebook page as a social community that supports your business. Many fans of your page will be friends who are not customers, but can still favorably influence the online reputation of your business.

- Be sure you have at least three administrators for your Facebook business page because personal accounts that provide access to your page can get deleted and are often unrecoverable.

- Edit your page settings to establish the most appropriate category for your page; Facebook will use that to locate your business in their search results.

- You can edit your settings to receive e-mail notifications when someone comments on your page.

- When the phone rings, the caller expects an answer; the same applies to your Facebook page or profile. Respond to comments to the extent that it is appropriate. For example, off topic and extraneous comments are usually better left alone.

- Make it a habit to "like" the comments that others make on your page or personal profile. By acknowledging them in this way, you're sending a social signal back to Facebook, thereby increasing the likelihood of those people receiving your content in the future.

- Pin your best posts (edit setting in upper right corner of post) to the top of your Facebook business page to profile your best content—especially during peak business times when you are expecting special visitors.

- Post as frequently as necessary to generate the desired level of engagement. Depending upon your community, this could range from once or twice a week to multiple times per day. It will take some experimentation to keep your business engaged with your community. A sure indicator is when interaction falls off—this is usually a sign of too little, too much, or irrelevant sharing.

LINKEDIN

There are many interesting contrasts between Facebook and LinkedIn, a site that now exceeds over 200 million users worldwide. Unlike Facebook, LinkedIn is completely searchable by users, and much of its content is readily indexed by Google. In fact, one of the easiest ways to learn more about a business connection is to simply Google their name followed by the words "on LinkedIn." This will take you to their personal profile, where you can learn more. Just be advised that people will know you visited their profile unless you adjust your settings to be anonymous, which is only possible with the premium versions.

LinkedIn redesigned their LinkedIn Company pages by borrowing a few features from Facebook and Twitter. The pages have a friendly look and feel that resembles a Facebook page, and page owners can receive notifications of comments made to their timeline posts. Additionally, businesses can profile products and services on their home page.

Many businesses are going all in on Facebook because that is where they can most easily connect with their friends. However, LinkedIn is quietly making strong moves, and its business focus and continued enhancements definitely merit more of your attention.

Best Practices

- LinkedIn is *the* network for business professionals. Regular updates to your LinkedIn profile keep it fresh—and that keeps you and your business relevant with everyone in your network.

- You should periodically save your LinkedIn connections to your CRM—Customer Relationship Manager.

- Because LinkedIn is searchable, you should use keywords in your heading, titles, and pretty much all of the content within your personal profile and pages.

- Even when LinkedIn says your profile is 100 percent complete, there is still more you can do to make it stronger. Explore the applications within LinkedIn and consider subscribing to the LinkedIn blog or joining a group focused on making the most of LinkedIn.

- Consider a LinkedIn request to connect as you would an exchange of business cards at any networking event. There is no commitment to necessarily engage, but the potential is nevertheless there.

TWITTER

Twitter is an extremely powerful network that delivers news around the world in real time. The short-burst 140-character message limit encourages speed, as does the practice of "retweeting"—that is, republishing a message originally posted by someone else to share with your followers.

Regardless of the number of followers you have, it's safe to assume that your Twitter news sharing and conversations will be seen by the world. That's the power of retweeting. Even celebrities who should be more media savvy have tweeted certain statements that have put them in uncomfortable situations—in some cases, even significantly altering their careers.

Used responsibly, Twitter can be invaluable for a business that understands how to capitalize on a big stage to showcase what they do well. It has earned a reputation as a credible source of timely news, and it tends to be actively used by most social media power users.

Best Practices

- The key to getting the most out of Twitter is engagement and sharing. If you continuously blast marketing messages, you will only prompt people to stop following you.

- Keep your tweets to less than 120 characters to allow space for the Twitter address of the person retweeting your message.

- Real-time search is a significant trend, and many of the emerging social search engines acquire their content from Twitter. So, you should be aware of judiciously using relevant keywords and hashtags to enhance your messages for search. (Hashtags are keyword phrases preceded by the # symbol to make them readily searchable.)

- You can set your Twitter settings to receive notifications on your mobile device whenever you receive direct messages or @mentions (tweets addressed directly to you).

- Use Twitter lists to better focus and personalize your communications for specific communities, including creating a list of current and prospective customers.

GOOGLE+

While Google+ is often considered to be Google's social network—and an answer to Facebook—Google has been positioning it as something more. They now prefer to represent Google+ as an "identity service"—something that it accomplishes by merging social marketing data from across numerous Google properties (such as YouTube, Picassa, and Google maps)—as well as from many other websites and networks.

In addition to steady growth of activity on Google+, it also has the strength of Google behind it. It is clear that Google is making Google+ the linchpin that could eventually connect all of its services. For example, when Google imported all of the Google Places for Business into Google+ and renamed them Google+ Local, it effectively encouraged 80 million businesses to join Google+.

Best Practices

- Google+ users organize their communities with circles. In addition to the circles you choose, Public is another choice that makes your sharing visible to the Google search engine. You will find this by clicking on "More" when making your post.

- Your Google+ profile is an opportunity to aggregate all of the sources where you publish online content, thereby enhancing your online identity and authorship of original content. Take the time to include these links to make that content more readily available to Google, and establish your Google Authorship to enhance the search ranking of your original content.

- The Google+ equivalent of a Facebook Like is the "+1." It's a vote of confidence that sends a social signal that you like this content. The share button allows you to share that content with your respective circles.

- Just as you can follow anyone on Twitter, you can place anyone in your circles on Google+ to learn more about people, specific industries, and businesses.

- When you write your bio for your "About" page, be sure to include links to your website and other relevant sites including blogs and other social networks. This is a powerful use of Google+ for SEO—it is practically a direct line for informing Google where you are active on the web.

YOUR BLOG

It is essential to understand that you cannot control your content on the respective social channels—you have no ownership, only free rent. This is why it is wise to protect and preserve your content to the extent that you are able, and the ideal way to do this is with a self-hosted blog on a domain that you own. Make that your social media hub—one that you will control and own for life. Then use the other networks for what they do best: sharing and engagement. (For more on blogging, see Chapters 3 and 8, and Appendix: Online Resources.)

SUSTAINABLE BUSINESS IS THE BY-PRODUCT OF ENGAGED COMMUNITIES

Businesses that are fully engaged with their communities learn to pivot and respond to the changing needs of those communities. An engaged business is surrounded by social signals that provide clues for making the necessary adjustments to keep the business on track and relevant within the future context of the community ecosystem. These social signals include casual conversations on the street, persistent concerns about a particular product or service, and even a nod that indicates gratitude for a job well done. In other words, any kind or source of information helps your business know whether it's on or off course. The trick is being aware of the subtle social signals.

DIGITAL SOCIAL SIGNALS

Social media provides small and large businesses alike the opportunity to learn from digital social signals. A social signal in the real world is a smile or a genuine compliment, whereas it is a like or share on Facebook, an endorsement on LinkedIn, or a retweet or favorite on Twitter in the digital world. All of these provide clues to people's preferences.

Social signals let you know how your products are really being used—something you need to know.

CUSTOMERS LEAD MARKET CHANGES

What blindsides most businesses is the fact that change can be slow. Change is happening every single day; the challenge is to be tuned in enough to discern these changes, so the business can adapt accordingly. The business leads the change in a product-driven market; however, customers lead the change in community-driven markets.

As discussed earlier in this chapter, businesses have traditionally used methods such as market research to look for changing market conditions and behaviors. Unfortunately, the information acquisition process creates a number of challenges. For example, responses will vary according to the questions asked, who is asking the questions, and how they are doing that—and even the physical environment. This is complicated by the fact that the data may no longer be relevant by the time it is compiled.

While there has always been an abundance of information available from sales professionals, this information rarely finds its way up the management ranks. And even if it does, it's not always considered trustworthy because sales representatives tend to filter and shape it to their benefit. This is why management wants to hear directly from the customer.

And now they can. Customer preferences are playing out every day on the social networks, and leading businesses are using a variety of monitoring tools to take full advantage of this real-time data. Small businesses should at the very least be using Google Alerts (Google.com/alerts) to monitor their business brand and key community influences, which may include a few competitors, civic leaders, and related or allied businesses.

To be more proactive, it is essential to recognize that any involvement by the business can influence the information source. That is to say that some people will tell you what they believe you want to know. Your business needs to be aware of this and learn how to effectively remove the business from the process in order to get the most honest feedback.

One of the best methods for doing so is to ask a lot of questions and look for patterns. We will all eventually speak the truth, given the opportunity, as long as there is no risk. For example: What do you think you are going to hear if you ask a customer if they are getting a good value? They may suspect that an affirmative response will result in a price increase in the future. It's better to ask in a way that keeps everything from getting personal, with a question such as: "Do you think others would say we provide good value?" What they think about their situation will follow.

If you really want to smoke out what is on the minds of your customers before they start looking for the door, you need to ask good questions—the ones that nobody else is asking them, such as: "Would you pay more for a better product?" A "yes" reply suggests that your quality may not be where it needs to be.

Being a community-minded business is to be interested in the people in your communities—and that makes your business interesting to them. Use these social channels well to ensure the future relevancy of your business by engaging with the people it serves.

Try This: Make One Weekly Improvement

If you make just one weekly improvement to one of the major social networks, you will leapfrog over your peers in social marketing capabilities.

All of us can always do more—and that is overwhelming given the ongoing changes and enhancements to these platforms.

Regardless of your current level of sophistication, commit to implementing one of the best practices suggested in this chapter.

- Choose one practice for each network to get started. That will keep you busy for one month, which is how long it should take to build this habit of steady improvement.
  - Facebook
  - LinkedIn
  - Google+
  - Twitter
- Choose a day of the week to make these improvements and schedule them into your calendar to build the habit—or work with a staff member to handle the implementation.
- Share the progress at your weekly team meeting.

CHAPTER 5

Meet Your New
Business Partners

As consumers move online in greater numbers, their collective voice will get even stronger, creating disruption in every community, business sector, and industry.

Businesses have successfully operated for generations on the strength of quality products and exceptional customer service. That just isn't enough anymore in a connection economy that introduces new dynamics that are impacting business success, namely, the relationship the business has with its customers, employees, and other community influencers—even competitors.

Social networks are connecting all of us in ways we never could have imagined. As a result, interrelationships are becoming opportunity drivers for communities. A community is more than people, organizations, and institutions in a physical location. It is a living phenomenon that is appropriately perceived as an ecosystem—a fluid, dynamic, and integrated environment in which the whole depends upon the components for its success. If you don't work with the system, you may find it working against you and your business.

Not only is a business not sustainable without loyal customers, it also needs the support of employees, advocates, and the general community at large. Call them what you wish—but if you view your business relationships as partners, you will always be better oriented to maximize the potential of those relationships.

COOPERATION IN THE CONNECTION ECONOMY

Influence in the business world has traditionally been centralized within institutions; that gave them the power to control how their organization interacts with the marketplace. In a connection economy that power is spread across all ranks, including customers, employees, and competitors. The challenge for businesses is learning how to work with their new connections, effectively making them allies or partners.

Our connected world is moving toward greater interdependencies, which means cooperation will become a necessary skill for success, both locally and globally. If you take a moment to consider all of the resources you need to operate your business, you will realize you are impacted every day by the influences of people, events, and circumstances around the globe.

For example, did you know that 97 percent of the world's available supply of rare earth metals—a family of elements necessary for the production of hybrid vehicles, power generating windmills, and the mobile devices you use every day—is located within China? Every local ecosystem is part of a larger one, and then another still larger, until ultimately the realization dawns that we indeed are all connected in ways we may not yet realize.

Forward thinking businesses are realizing that in this connection economy it makes practical sense to partner with others to multiply your strengths. On a local level these are the people with whom your business is already closely aligned, including customers, employees, and other local businesses that may or may not be competitors.

Your business should not have to look too far to discover opportunities for partnering, and we'll discuss in this chapter a number of ways that can be accomplished. The starting point is recognizing that partnering not only makes your business stronger, it has an equal or greater effect on the communities that support it.

COLLABORATION MAKES EVERYONE BETTER

In a business environment where customers have come to expect quality and competitive pricing, people are the differentiating factor. Social networking has the potential to make every individual that touches your business a partner that contributes to its success. The challenge is to leverage the strength of these combinations to jointly accomplish the respective needs of everyone concerned.

When you consider everyone in your network, you realize that your business has enormous upside potential if you simply connect the dots to the friends of your friends. That is the true power of your social network—building a bridge from what may only be hundreds of first-level network connections creates the potential for meeting the thousands of second-level connections to whom they can introduce you.

One of the first steps for multiplying your social network is to align your business with employees who will willingly share their joy of working for your business. The clients I work with are often amazed at what happens when they simply involve their trusted staff to reach out to their friends. They see how quickly it can advance the mission of the business that, of course, supports them and their family. If you have a solid company culture, this kind of initiative powerfully reminds everyone that they are capable of making a significant contribution to the success of the business.

Employees

After decades of small business ownership, I have learned that if you really want to have happy customers, you only need to hire good people who share values similar to yours. While talent is undeniably valuable, it is not nearly as important in daily situations as the desire to be a team player that has the interests of the business at heart.

In order for your employees to help your company, they have to enjoy both their work and the people with whom they spend their workdays. When you have loyal employees that treat the business as if it were their own, you have new partners that will willingly spread the message of the good work it does. All you have to do is give them permission to use the social networks to do so.

If this is true for your business, you already have a tribe that is sharing with all of their friends in their respective niches within the community, which may include some that you are not even familiar with. This kind of word-of-mouth promotion proved to be invaluable for the success of my landscape business—long before the advent of social media. We all came from very different backgrounds and attracted customers from our respective social circles. I can only imagine how much more powerful that could have been if social networking had been available. Smart businesses are recognizing this trend, and paying more attention to candidates with impressive online social networks.

Customers

One of the underlying principles of the web is that it works to serve consumers first and businesses second. Therefore, as consumers move online in greater numbers, their collective voice will get even stronger, thereby creating disruption in every community, business sector, and industry.

This is why it is essential for your business to not only use social media, but to design your company around its influences. As we know, customer service is no longer a one-to-one conversation with you and your customer. It now takes place in an online public forum. Though this reality scares some businesses, it is a reality nonetheless and one to which we all must adapt. Fortunately, it's not that difficult to do so.

If you are using social media primarily to broadcast your business message, you have undoubtedly noticed that it is merely background noise compared to the increasingly powerful voice of socially engaged consumers. Your challenge is to leverage that power by favorably engaging it with your business brand.

If your business is taking good care of your customers, then they're likely sharing the value they derive from your business with their friends. However, it is always wise to occasionally ask them if they will share positive comments with their social networking communities. Many small businesses that are otherwise using social media will miss this critical step of making a simple call to action to get the community to act on their behalf.

Before social media, my best clients gladly offered to do media interviews for newspaper editorials about our business, despite the fact that it was a significant investment of their time. Compared to that, asking someone to share an occasional tweet or Facebook comment is a very reasonable request. If you make it a policy to ask, you will be pleasantly surprised by the response. Of course, you do have to keep in mind that some customers value their privacy, and that has to be respected.

Influencers

If you operate a small business, it is possible that some people—such as a spouse, or former customers—bring you business, despite the fact that they are not officially on your payroll. We even had potential customers sending us business—people that could not afford our services but had friends who could. All of these connections are influencers and can contribute significantly to your business success.

One problem is that it can be difficult to remain in touch with people that you are only loosely connected with. Now, however, you can leverage the power of social media—not only to stay in touch with these influencers, but to connect with new ones. As your circle of friends and followers grows, you will find it valuable to use lists and tags to organize your communities so that you can occasionally reach out to them.

If you operate a local business, you have friends in the local community who are invaluable business partners. Use social media to remind them that you are alive, well, and ready to serve your community, both as a citizen and a business. This isn't marketing in a traditional sense, but confident pride of ownership and service to the community. And that's worthy of being shared if you present it well.

Influencers can sometimes do more for your online marketing than you can imagine. A few of my influential acquaintances appreciate the content I publish on my blog; when they share it with their communities the effect is nothing short of amazing. You simply cannot underestimate the influence of one person with a loyal tribe, and how that can sometimes magically work to help your business prosper.

Competitors

The true competitors for most businesses are their own fears about outside conditions or influences.

Consider whether any of the following statements sound familiar:

- "They stole our idea."

- "Our quality is much better."

- "Those low-ballers cut the price again."

These are unfortunately the responses you will hear from businesses that are stuck—they are trying to hold on to how things used to be instead of adapting. Leading companies are a lot like successful salespeople in that they notice obstacles and failures just long enough to learn from them—and then use them to innovate. One of the most pervasive trends in business today is using social media to personalize your business to open doors that are only open to friends, thereby eliminating the competition entirely.

In that regard, consider who knows nearly as much about your business as you do—your competitors. They also know just as much (or more) about your industry and markets as you do. You can identify these organizations and people; and if you can trust them, doesn't it make sense to have conversations to explore potential opportunities? You will find differences when you look for them—just as you will also discover opportunities for developing beneficial partnerships if you are open to them as well.

One precaution is to be aware that there are regulations to protect free markets. When talking with your competition, be sure you understand the laws regarding issues such as restraint of trade and other forms of collusion. These laws have serious penalties designed to protect the community, so do your homework to learn more about the relevant regulations in your industry, region, and country, such as the Robinson-Patman and Clayton Acts here in the United States.

BUSINESS PARTNERING IS THE NEW LEADERSHIP

Viewing competitors as potential partners starts with adopting a mindset of cooperation as opposed to competition. There is, by definition, a winner and a loser when you are competing. When you are partnering, however, everyone shares in the favorable outcome. The only way to have losers in that scenario is to create a complete failure, which is unlikely to occur when there is true cooperation.

The key to successful partnerships is to take them one project at a time. This allows you to limit your risk to a single endeavor. Think of it like a first date; if it doesn't work out, everyone moves on. If it does, you can consider another. If things in your business feel "stuck" this may be just what you need to move it forward—partnering with another company with complementary strengths.

You will notice more partnering taking place in virtually every industry to share both risk and the rewards. Trade associations in particular are combining resources to work together on events and legislative efforts while still retaining their respective memberships. This approach maximizes the benefits to members, while also driving down the costs for delivering them.

The new model is all about inclusiveness. Working together to better serve markets and communities creates better solutions that sustain businesses. If you are open to this you are already on the right track for using social marketing to align your business with more demanding customer expectations.

For example, to accomplish large-scale construction projects during a limited window of time, it's not uncommon in many industries to combine the efforts of several established companies working as one, sometimes with the help of a firm focused solely on managing the project. This was occasionally a practice in the landscape industry when large corporate campus projects were built. The combined resources for more quickly digging, transporting, and installing plantings during cooler temperatures optimally provided time for them to acclimate to their new environment before punishing summer conditions arrived.

Exercise your leadership qualities to initiate discussions for combining your resources, experience, and industry knowledge with like-minded professionals. You can better serve your customers without taking on unnecessary overhead that has put many companies out of business. Business today is more challenging than ever—especially for small enterprises whose resources are already stretched. Cooperation is replacing competition, and that's a good thing for businesses and customers alike.

A Familiar Model for Partnerships

Partnerships do not have to be a marriage. As discussed previously, they can exist for a sufficient duration to advance a single project. This approach is actually a model commonly used for creating major motion pictures. From the director and actors to the studio and financial investors, everyone has a specific reason for being involved.

Making a film is a project that has a defined beginning, middle, and end—and when the project is complete, everyone goes their own way. As a landscape contractor, we were used to thinking in terms of projects. Doing this is invaluable for creating intense focus to effectively mobilize and then employ resources for accomplishing a well-designed objective.

Project work is tangible. The roles are defined, and everyone is committed to their role and its value for achieving the desired end result. Everyone on a film set plays a part. Some are more prominent than others; some are temporary, and others will endure for the entire project. Some actors may even quit or get fired. Yet the film is nearly always produced despite the drama that happens behind the scenes. It's no different than your day-to-day business activities.

The filmmaking model may help you get more comfortable with the concept of business partnering. It's an approach that emphasizes the fact that it's all about getting a job done—it does not necessarily have to be a long-term relationship. Special event companies especially are familiar with this model, because to keep their events fresh they seek new venues and talent from one year to the next—which results in a new mix of players aligned for the purpose of being relevant to the audience they serve. Contrast this with the traditional view of the business as an enterprise—a corporation that will last into eternity. As most of us know all too well, the forever business entity concept is a thing of the past.

Any small business owner knows that employees come and go; and unfortunately, the same holds true for some customers and suppliers. Thus, it's best to think of your business not as an enterprise, but rather as a collaboration for best accomplishing what you can today. Make the most of the resources at hand, including all of those potential business partners within your network that can help you advance your business objectives.

GIVE THEM SOMETHING TO TALK ABOUT

People talk—and now, with social media, they share photos and videos, too. You want to give them something to talk about that favorably speaks to your business merits. This obviously involves caring for your customers exceptionally well and encouraging them to share those experiences. But unless you are a mainstream consumer brand, this alone won't provide enough material to keep the conversation alive.

Recall from Chapter 1 that searching for solutions to common problems is what drives the web. To that end, being the go-to source of relevant solutions in your industry is one of the most powerful ways to assure that people are frequently talking about your business online. This opportunity is still wide open in every community, for the simple reason that the best solutions are often local, and the majority of local businesses have yet to embrace content marketing.

It's time for that to change—and you can be part of facilitating this change. If you are a small business, with decades of experience and local customers, you are ideally equipped to be a content-marketing leader in your community, and quite possibly in your industry as well. Your direct experience with the community is relatable, and is invaluable to buyers who want to minimize risk.

In buying situations where there is risk—which is many of them—content from trustworthy community insiders will naturally be considered the most valuable. This "wisdom of friends" that is occasionally a by-product of Facebook is more readily found within focused community and industry blogs. Develop the practice of blogging; give your communities a reason to share commentary that is a direct result of your interactions with local customers.

Just because a business is local does not mean it understands the local community. For example, while some national chains may have brick and mortar locations in our communities, their staff has limited historical experience with its members. This creates opportunities for local businesses that do have that information—what many refer to as *local knowledge*.

Golfers use this term to describe the subtle ways the greens respond to a putt, or how the prevailing winds will tend to shape a shot. In a friendly match, these subtleties can make a big difference, and are therefore highly valued. Over time, truly local businesses learn similar nuances about the buying behaviors of their customers—information that allows them to earn their continued loyalty.

Customers quickly gravitate toward businesses that they perceive care about them, and the easiest way to create that perception is to put their needs first. This means being a friendly and trusted source of information that helps them make better buying decisions.

Anyone that has a vested interest in your business is a viable partner, and that obviously includes customers. The challenge for businesses is engaging and involving community members to the extent that they feel they have partnership stake in the success of your business. Customers usually understand that if your business does well, they will in turn share in your prosperity. Mostly they just like to be acknowledged as being part of it.

You can accomplish this directly with them, or by giving back to the community. Ideally, your business should have a plan in place for doing both. Most people are more interested in being genuinely appreciated. You will be amazed at what the gift of a few kind words on your social channels will do to get your community talking favorably about your business. Try it.

FROM PRODUCT TO COMMUNITY MANAGEMENT

When I graduated from college in the early 1980s, the top marketing jobs outside of Wall Street were in product or brand management and advertising. Consumer product companies especially placed a great deal of emphasis on cultivating their brands. They worked closely with outside advertising agencies to help them enhance the awareness of these brand identities.

A brand is like a persona; it's a projection of who you think your audience wants you to be—an effort to be cool. In our world of greater transparency, people will tend to make their own conclusions about what is cool based upon the information available to them. In that respect, they have a great deal of influence over the identity and reputation of business brands in the marketplace.

Communities are the new markets—and they know what they want. This is why smart businesses are embracing the practice of community management—engaging with communities to help them do more of what hasn't been done that will better meet their challenges and opportunities.

About a year after I started my landscape company, a large upscale subdivision was built and there were few capable companies in the area doing residential landscape maintenance back then, which was clearly in demand. We responded to this need by investing in a new truck, trailer, and all of the necessary equipment to maintain just a handful of homes, but knowing there were 600 more homes to be built. A few years later we were operating four crews and managing nearly 150 properties in that community; it was the result of simply learning the needs of that particular community—and doing what hadn't been done by our competitors up until then.

When a business focuses as much on the community as it does its products and services, it learns valuable information that helps to build a better business brand. Apple has a great deal of brand loyalty for their successful innovations, but their retail stores that serve as a lifeline for connected consumers may well be their greatest innovation. It is comforting for Apple product owners to know that there are helping hands available seven days a week if anything goes wrong with their computing devices.

There is without question a similar solution just waiting to be developed in your industry or community. The better you understand the communities you serve, the more likely your business will learn what hasn't been done—something that can literally eliminate the competition when you create it.

Creative advertising and sexy marketing is what used to make a brand cool. Apple became cool by giving people what they desperately wanted: the opportunity to buy innovative products from knowledgeable sales professionals and technicians in a welcoming environment that is so engaging it became a social phenomenon. You can do the same.

COMMUNITY MANAGEMENT RESPONSIBILITIES

Managing your online communities can be an overwhelming undertaking—even to the point that it distracts your attention from your core business activities. However, if you establish basic guidelines and work as a team with your new business partners, you will discover it can actually be a rewarding and enjoyable experience that serves your business well.

After conducting considerable research on leading online community guidelines, my current business settled on the following three guidelines for our online communities:

1. Be yourself.
2. Respect others.
3. Add value.

To be clear, these are community guidelines for everyone that participates in our communities—with my blog being the one that is primary. My blog is my social media hub, a site where I have complete ownership and control. For that reason, I believe that I have a greater responsibility for ensuring everyone feels welcome and safe to express their views there.

I have other personal guidelines for myself, one of which includes avoiding the need to be right. One of my primary social media objectives is to learn from the community—something that's only possible if I am receptive to new perspectives with which I may not initially agree. My belief is that every opinion has potential for adding value if it is presented in a way that respects other community members.

I'm occasionally asked about the legal implications of having such a loose community management policy. It's always an option to consult with an attorney if you feel you need to; but be prepared for things to get complicated if you do. Attorneys are trained to protect you from what can go wrong, and we all know that is just about everything. Whereas, maintaining awareness of the overall well-being of a community is a policy that works well and is easily managed.

A viable and proven solution for addressing community management is to ground it within a set of core values. If the culture of a business is strong, then it will provide the structure to account for numberless unforeseen situations. This is how giant online retailer Zappos has managed their social media from the beginning, and it has worked exceptionally well for them.

Zappos does not have an official social media policy, other than adhering to the ten core company values that guide the behavior of thousands of employees. And since hundreds of them are actively participating in social media, we know that it can't be—and doesn't have to be—all that complicated.

What to Do About Negative Comments?

Depending upon the community you are managing, you may or may not be able to delete inappropriate comments or block objectionable community members. In light of increased oversight and concerns for privacy and security, this control will likely become a required option on every major social network. However, one should be careful about exercising too much control, since this risks discouraging spirited conversations that may prove to be productive and encourage more engagement. Respectful disagreement should be allowed.

It is vital for your business to respond to comments that reflect negatively on it or anyone associated with it. You have to acknowledge these and attempt to clarify any false perceptions. Seek to guide the conversation to higher ground. However, understand that some people enjoy the sport of trolling. They are actually looking for opportunities to instigate arguments, and at some point you have to just let go—or let them go.

You'll discover that community behavior will tend to follow leadership. Having core values that you visibly display and lead by will encourage desirable behavior. Make it a point to periodically remind the community of your community values and guidelines. This was something I learned from Copyblogger.com, an Internet marketing community with a passion for copywriting, blogging, and content marketing.

During the early days of blogging it was not uncommon for conversations to get out of hand, something that is still common today on YouTube and the major news sites because it goes unchecked. When this would happen at Copyblogger, the leadership would address it and refer the community to the published guidelines. Over time the disrespectful behavior disappeared, most likely because they found another place to practice.

When there is undesirable behavior, it is always best to firmly, but carefully, address it. Demonstrate your willingness to understand what is on the individual's mind if they respect the decorum of the community. Some people are not skilled communicators or simply don't know how to throttle their energies, which is why the role of the community manager is so vital.

Try This: Explore Partnerships

You will find these guidelines to be helpful when considering new partnering opportunities.

- Find partners you can trust. Proceed no further until you are comfortable with whom you plan to work together with.

- Find partners whose style matches yours. It is important to work with partners that provide complementary strengths; however, their working style should be similar to yours.

- Share the work—separate the responsibilities. If you share responsibilities and your partner is not able to perform, your business will have to carry the entire load—and maybe still split the profits.

- Design a small project to test the partnership. Since trust is so important, it is often smart to choose a low-risk project just to test the working styles of the partnership. If everything works well you can take your working relationship to a higher level.

CHAPTER 6

Business Is Now Personal

When you reduce social media to nothing more than a checkbox, you lose the one thing that makes it work—you.

Small business owners tend to wear many hats—something that usually leaves them little time for strategic activities that have a longer payoff. Instead of blogging to build traffic to their website, they are more likely to be taking care of real customers. So, when they do have time for social media they tend to use it as another form of advertising to bring in more customers.

The irony is that the personal attention they give to their customers is often the one quality that is missing from their social marketing—one that will make the emotional connection that is necessary for it to resonate with their audience. The surest way to drive traffic to your website is to use social marketing to amplify your personal qualities—especially those that make you more authentic. The traditional marketing mindset can be a tough habit to break, but it is essential if you want to understand how social marketing really works.

Why, you may wonder, would people want to know about you personally? That depends upon a number of factors that we all have to answer for ourselves. You may not get the answers you are looking for, but you nevertheless have to give it a shot to learn how to engage people with your business.

Fortunately, there are ways to personalize your business while also maintaining whatever level of privacy you may desire. For example, author Seth Godin readily admits he is uncomfortable sharing details about his family life online. Yet, everyone who's been following this prolific blogger for over a decade has a strong sense of who he is as a person. It comes out in his writing. When you make social media a regular practice your personal qualities will naturally come through.

Look at this from a customer's perspective. When you receive outstanding service, you are more likely to recommend not just the company, but the person within it who was responsible for your favorable experience. That's the power of personalization, and it's what makes the experience so memorable. The company itself is often incidental. What matters is the one person who made a difference for you. That human touch anchors both that person and the company they represent in your memory for some time to come—and it works exactly the same with social media.

This chapter is divided into three segments for using personalization that mirrors the organization and design of this book: first earn the attention of those in your community; then engage them; and ultimately collaborate with them to learn if there is common ground for doing business together. It's a process of being relatable, engaging, and then thoughtful enough to help people with your available business resources.

PERSONALIZATION MAKES YOUR BUSINESS MEMORABLE

Social media is conditioning consumers to expect businesses to behave with transparency and full disclosure. They also want access to key decision makers. If you are the business owner or a leading manager, this means you. This trend will become even more prevalent as the generation that grew up with Facebook continues to join the workforce.

It is a fact that most people have been conditioned not to trust companies—at least until they get to know them. Developing trust is easily accomplished by pulling back the curtain. Take your customers behind the scenes to get to know your company through the people that make it all happen. It only takes one favorable experience with anyone in your business to build a valuable relationship with a member of your community. Of course, this connection can be even more powerful if that member of your company happens to be one of its leaders.

Small business leaders are quasi-celebrities in their local communities. This is a quality that you should attempt to capitalize on with your social marketing. It gives people confidence and pride to be working with the owner. While this becomes increasingly challenging as your business grows, it is still possible to stay connected with everyone in your community through Facebook, LinkedIn, or even your personal or company blog. All of these channels assure customers that they have a direct line to the top should they care to use it. And though most probably never will, simply knowing they have the ability to do so is enough for it to work in your favor.

Personalization is your strongest business differentiator, and social media helps you to extend and amplify that through your own accounts and those of your team members. The crucial distinction is that personalization happens between two people—not one person and a business. You therefore ideally want to have active personal profiles on all of the major social networks. Some people choose not to do so, and that is a personal decision, but limiting your exposure will restrict your social marketing effectiveness.

Personal versus Business Social Media Accounts

If your business has abundant resources to manage many social media profiles, then choosing to focus on personal versus business accounts may be a little easier. You can set up personal and business accounts on multiple social networks to test the social media waters, choosing later where to focus the efforts of your team, which may include hiring a media agency to help if you are a larger business.

The reality, however, is that resources are limited for most of us—which narrows the focus on how many accounts we can effectively manage. One thing is certain: it is better to actively use one account well than to have dozens that receive little or no attention. Of course, as discussed in Chapter 3, it is wise to maintain a distributed presence to buffer against the inevitable future changes to the respective networks.

A primary objective of social media is engaging an audience—which can be challenging for a faceless business or brand. People like to know who they are having a social media conversation with for a variety of reasons. They may wish to know your background out of pure curiosity, your longevity with the business for purposes of relevancy, or your perceived level of authority for getting things done on their behalf. While all of these considerations are important, the most essential is putting a friendly face out in front of the business—not side by side with the logo, but clearly out front and more prominent.

Companies that enjoyed early success with social media were the ones who quickly learned the value of having one individual in front of their big business brand. Scott Monty with Ford Motor Company is one notable example. Scott is well known within social media circles as "Scott Monty who works for Ford"—as opposed to Ford's social media leader Scott Monty. The distinction of being a person first is vital, because that is the magnetic or attraction element that ultimately humanizes the brand. It stands to reason that this approach is even more relevant for businesses in local communities where customers can readily identify the owner, or any other visible representatives of the company.

Your customers—and your community in general—think of your social marketing business accounts as the company, just as they would your website. The distinction is that a website is static and typically nonsocial, whereas a social networking account is expected to be both social and interactive. Thus, you must skillfully and consistently manage your social marketing presence to provide whatever it is that customers may expect from your business. Hosting the social marketing accounts presents responsibilities for which many smaller businesses may not be ready—which explains why their blogs and business pages are not generating the sales leads or engagement they desire.

Think of every single online business site or profile in the same way you do your business cards, trucks, or uniforms—as a reflection of your business. They should be nicely designed, clean, well maintained—and of course, actively managed. Are you prepared to be available to field important questions about your business? How about taking 15 minutes or more out of your busy day to chat with a customer that just wants to say hello and share their experience with your company? It all comes with the territory.

In contrast, a personal profile comes with very different and more easily managed expectations. For one thing, you are not expected to have your company hat on 100 percent of the time. This frees you up to just learn about people and get to know them on a level where you can truly be friends. That provides immeasurable power for then engaging with their tribe, individuals who may—like them—also have an interest in working with your business. Don't ever forget how the social graphs (Chapter 1) work to facilitate this—connecting you to the expansive networks of those whose trust you have earned.

It should now be clear that you want to lead with active personal accounts if you are serious about social marketing and really want to harness its full value. Unfortunately, businesses are often scrambling to do exactly the opposite, taking a business as usual approach that has a counterproductive effect. And because many of their peers are doing the same thing, it all goes largely unnoticed. If everybody is doing it and nobody is getting results, it stands to reason that it is probably not the right approach for your business.

Personal Is Relatable and Trustworthy

Unlike traditional advertising campaigns, social marketing takes time to do its job. This is one reason why many small businesses throw in the towel on their efforts, and revert back to the traditional practices that worked in the past—right when they may be approaching the threshold of achieving practical results. They view social media as another form of advertising that is expected to deliver results now. This creates the temptation to set up business pages on every social network to drive traffic to their websites. If you have already done this you may wish to consider taking some of them down, because abandoned accounts on the web give the same impression to customers as vacant properties do in real life.

Traditional marketing tends to highlight distinctions between competitors that may or may not be true. Some of these claims include being the best, the most awarded, and so on. As a result, consumers have learned not to trust advertising. Their experience tells them that if something seems too good to be true—it probably is. This is why virtually every claim today is challenged by those who use the Internet to validate what they have learned from other sources—including word-of-mouth recommendations from friends.

What are they looking for? Not more traditional marketing—that's for sure. Consumers are searching the web for reliable information from real people who offer perspectives that are backed by their direct experience. This is the power of content marketing—combining valid experience and credible information to bring an element of truthfulness to the marketing equation.

Have you ever been unsatisfied and ready to discontinue your relationship with a business, only to change your mind based on the actions of one especially thoughtful company representative? Just like that, one person was able to single-handedly regain your trust in the business—and that is memorable. This is why putting a face on the business is so powerful. How many of us have ever said we "never forget a face"? In a business environment where people regularly receive poor or average service, extraordinary customer service is newsworthy. It's the kind of thing that people tend to share on the social networks, so it is helpful if they can personally connect with that person online to applaud them.

To encourage more engagement on social networks, you will want to be careful about patterning your every move after what other businesses are doing. In business there is a tendency to follow the herd—which is fine if the herd is moving in the right direction. However, many businesses are mostly thinking about—and operating according to—what they want. You can distinguish your business by being the one that innovates to give the customer what they want. That starts by being relatable—more like them than your competitors.

It can take years for some businesses to earn the necessary trust for converting prospects into customers. To accomplish their goals, they have to keep them coming back for more, and the only way to do that is to be memorable and trusted. Social marketing personalization builds relatable and trustworthy connections that customers don't easily forget.

LOCAL BUSINESS LEADERS ARE TRUSTED CELEBRITIES

Even remarkable companies can fade away if they are not engaged with the communities they serve. Business requires leadership, and people naturally expect business leaders to be up front and personal in a socially connected business environment. While this has always been true, it is now more so than ever. New standards for success are developing in the business world, and an important one is the trustworthiness of companies and their leaders. It's an essential element in a society that has seen many companies and company heads fall due to compromising situations. People want to trust your business—and that starts with trusting you.

Google is becoming remarkably skilled at helping consumers locate just about anything with ease. This trend feeds our desire for more and better information about everything, including people. People will often search the web to learn more about someone with whom they are preparing to do business. The web makes even someone with a common name readily findable. If that person happens to be even the smallest kind of celebrity, a Wikipedia page will detail their life and accomplishments. And while most of us are not celebrities, we have likely had accomplishments as business leaders that put us on the radar of the searchable, social web.

True celebrities have brand influence based on trust earned from accomplishments in their area of expertise. Businesses hire them as spokespeople to endorse their brands; and in the process, they borrow the credibility and trust these individuals have earned. As a business leader, you too are a celebrity in your industry and community. You should therefore leverage your earned trust to personally endorse and support your own business, just as a celebrity would a major brand—skillfully using your personal charm.

Be aware that people are conducting searches for your name on sites such as LinkedIn, Twitter, and Google+. This makes you one of the essential ingredients for making your social marketing successful—provided you are personally engaged with your social marketing communities. When you reduce social media to nothing more than a checkbox, you lose the one thing that makes it work—you. You are the foundation of your company's social marketing presence, and everyone associated with it is a contributor as well.

It's interesting that the quality of personalization that is so vital to successful social marketing is the essential ingredient that many businesses tend to leave out of the mix. One explanation for this may be the idea that marketing is something you do to your markets to attract buyers. While that may be true, social marketing is something you do *with* your markets to remove any friction that may inhibit your working together.

THE FACEBOOK GENERATION EFFECT

One of the advantages of being older than many social marketing practitioners is the ability to apply decades of business experience to a new way of doing business—one that includes all of the social and new media technologies. Another is being able to have a front row seat to observe and learn from the behaviors and practices of those at the other end of the age spectrum.

My children and their generation were exposed to technology at a very young age. It began with the toys we gave them and continued with the computers they used in school. What is most significant is that they moved up to computers at the time that social media was just beginning to emerge. So, it should not be surprising that these recent high school and college graduates are part of a uniquely social generation. They grew up on Facebook, so they are inclined to be visible, join groups, and openly share. It is a natural extension of who they are, and it is sure to have an impact on our business environment as more of them join the workplace.

CONNECTED MICRO-COMMUNITY NETWORKS

Growing up with a platform like Facebook makes its use as natural for younger generations as the telephone was for the rest of us. We neither feared it, nor were in awe of its technological capabilities. We just used it to accomplish our objectives. My son used Facebook to select a compatible college roommate while he was still a high school senior. He later used it to organize friends from his hometown who would be attending the same out-of-state university, which of course later merged with the many new friends he would make. Once at college, his peers formed a Facebook group to better manage the social activities of the students that lived on the same floor of his co-ed dorm. This micro-community within the larger community of the university became close friends that year, and they still are to this day.

One lesson that businesses can draw from this is to organize your social communities for more relevant and personal interactions—while always keeping inclusivity in mind. Once a social community is defined, everyone within it is necessarily equal. This is a lesson that explains how social media not only democratizes media, but by extension, the business world that it influences.

Younger individuals have learned to use social media to intentionally include friends into their social circles, not necessarily to exclude others. Though this may seem to be an obvious distinction, it's an important one to make. Once you are included you are considered a trusted member of the community for as long as it may endure. This mindset of openness and inclusivity is one that younger employees will bring to the workplace. If your business does not share a similar philosophy, you may find yourself at odds with an entire generation of future workers. To be clear, they do respect social media privacy; however, they also honor the unwritten code that generally guides social media behaviors—intentional interaction that encourages teamwork—something we can all look forward to having more of in the workplace. Social networking for this generation is about organized community interaction.

THE TREND TOWARD OPEN ACCESS

If you are a small business owner expecting your new hires to be social media savvy, you will not be disappointed. However, you may be surprised to learn that while they can effectively use social media, they are not especially enamored with the tools and technology. As with prior generations and the telephone, they have used social media simply to accomplish specific objectives, such as organizing a social gathering. So, before making them the designated social media expert for your company, first consider if they really want that role.

In the film *Tin Cup*, a romantic comedy that takes place within the setting of the game of golf, one-time golf prodigy Roy McAvoy wins several wagers as a result of his technical golf skills, but he loses a major tournament due to making poor decisions. This generation has desirable technical skills too, when it comes to social media. However, like Roy McAvoy, they may not necessarily make the best decisions for any number of reasons. Thus, you will have to agree on ground rules for how your company likes to play the game of business, and how social marketing will be used to accomplish your objectives.

Just as you would not turn a sales professional loose without properly training them on how to work with your customers, you will need to do the same with your new recruits to encourage the right kind of community engagement. The Internet obviously gives us all access to both information and people, and this encourages similar expectations in real life. This is why your recent hires will also expect access to you from day one, both online and offline. They have this access now with their advisors, professors, and deans, and will be looking for that same interaction in the workforce.

Of course, this also means you will have to get over many of your fears with respect to social media privacy and what your staff is sharing on the social networks. Instead, your goal should be building a respectful culture, and then encouraging your team to freely use the social networks to share what they love about your company. Properly trained and led by example, these new business partners will engage your company with the supportive communities that already know and trust them.

COLLABORATION IS THE NEW MARKETING

When Ford CMO Jim Farley took the stage at the 2011 Blogworld Expo to share his thoughts about how his company is successfully implementing their social marketing, he communicated an important message—that it is effective only when every member of the organization, from the top down, practices it. He shared a thorough understanding of how this works, and in the process created an immediate connection with thousands of members of the blogging world who represent diverse communities.

Farley never suggested that we should like Ford, or that they had social marketing completely figured out. Instead, he made Ford likeable simply by sharing their challenges and successes—letting us draw our own conclusions. Farley's talk didn't feel like a presentation; rather, more like a conversation with colleagues. It highlighted that the very nature of social marketing is not a process of doing anything to the community; rather, it's one of collaborating with it to find the common ground that just may lead to a business relationship. It's definitely a slower process, but it's also one that is much more sustainable than other marketing methods when it starts working.

In many ways, the traditional marketing process is like living in an exclusive gated community and expecting to connect with the people outside of it. There are perceived barriers between businesses and the communities with whom they want to build relationships; yet, you can remove these barriers over time by actively engaging, sharing, and thereby personalizing your company.

Businesses possess valuable resources whose usefulness to their communities is often overlooked. For example, my landscape company owned dozens of trucks and trailers that were typically idle during the holiday season, so every Christmas we donated their use, along with some manpower, to transport gifts the community donated to needy families across town. It's a tradition we enjoyed immensely, and one I'm proud the company to whom I sold my business has continued. Smart businesses seek out these opportunities to share because it humanizes the business and connects the dots to new friends in the community.

Collaboration with a Purpose

To get what you want in business you need to consider the expectations of your target audience. In addition to customers, you may be seeking talented recruits—and the methods you use to attract them should be exactly the same as the ones you use for attracting new sales leads. It's a process of creating alignment with the desired community, and that starts with understanding them—and sharing useful information that demonstrates that understanding.

Whether you are trying to attract new customers or talented individuals to join your team, it may be helpful to examine how top colleges and universities encourage potential students to visit their campuses. They are no longer flooding the mailboxes of high school students with glossy brochures that depict an idyllic setting, a practice that dates back to when many of us were that age. According to one student, "It's annoying. Most of the stuff I get in the mail is like a picture of a kid. It's pretty useless."

These days savvier schools are using social media to personalize and engage with a very discerning crowd that is unresponsive to traditional marketing. "What we're trying to do with social media is be relatable and relevant," says Perry Hewitt, Harvard University's Chief Digital Officer. "In today's communications environment, it's not a ticket to win. It's a ticket to play." In other words, it is an opportunity to simply be in the game for what may happen when everyone works together.

Business is now personal, and social marketing is a surefire way to amplify the qualities that educated buyers of all ages are more likely to connect with. They've done their research and studied the relevant data; now they're seeking validation they can trust—relatable and relevant information that encourages buying behavior. As many parents know, their children get an intuitive feeling within minutes of stepping foot on a campus for the first time that tells them if they want to spend the next four years there. Your future buyers will get that same feeling about your business too, and it will generally be favorable if your social media effectively communicates a relatable under-standing about them; it has to be informative and sufficiently personalized to make an emotional connection.

To do this with social marketing you have to show your customers you speak their language and care about them, while reflecting all of that in appearance and form. In other words, your business has to be what it desires to attract. If you want to attract employees that are fun to work with, you need to show them your work environment is already upbeat and engaging. Our landscape business sought to attract creative designers and clients that appreciated innovative design. So, we reflected those qualities at every turn—starting with the artistic mosaic tile that greeted them when they first set foot into our lobby.

First impressions on the social networks are just as important. Use your understanding of your communities to create alignment that connects the dots to future opportunities. Since that's how it works in real life, it only stands to reason that it will work the same on the digital networks. As just noted, social marketing is a ticket to get into the game. Once you're in, you have to use your business acumen to convert that attention and engagement into practical results—which is the focus of Chapters 8, 9, and 10.

BEING A LIKEABLE BUSINESS

A few years ago, I was listening to a radio interview with Stan Lee, who is best known as a comic book writer and the former president and chairman of Marvel Comics. Lee created well-known figures like The Hulk, Iron Man, Captain America, and Spider Man. In this particular interview, Lee described how he created Spider Man—this insect of a man who was capable of scaling buildings.

He naturally considered names such as Insect Man, but he chose to go with Spider Man because of the strength it gave to the character. Then, however, he intentionally transformed Spider Man—the man—into a teenager. His reasoning for doing so was to make him vulnerable in ways that his predominantly teenage audience could relate to, and therefore making this character instantly more likeable.

Stan Lee not only showed his marketing brilliance with the final creation of Spider Man; he demonstrated an intimate understanding of his target audience and how to create a product that is relatable to them, and therefore, more likeable, too. To be a relevant business today, we all need to learn more about our customers. Thankfully, social media gives us the potential to do that by personally connecting with them on a human and emotional level.

Try This: Take Some Risks

Examine your social media profiles for the benefit of your audience—not for showing off.

- What are the one or two qualities that your community most wants from your business? Identify the keywords that describe them.
- Are these qualities (and the relevant keywords) evident in your profiles and the content you are sharing online?
  - Take some time with this—go back to your social channels and study whether your content is useful to your audience—or if it is more about you and your business.

How relatable are you?

- Is your profile photo recent and friendly?
- Are you talking like a friend or a business?

It is not easy for many of us to be personal online. Take a few small risks and evaluate the results over time.

PART THREE

Conversion: Transforming Trust into New Business

CHAPTER 7

Social and Local Are
Built-In Mobile

The intersection of social, local, and mobile is a marketing sweet-spot that is blurring the lines of time and place.

Mobile phones are much more than communication tools these days. They are practical computing devices that are revolutionizing how we live, work, and play—all of which is not going unnoticed by marketers. Searching the web and using it to connect with people used to focus on one variable—speed. But now that mobile technologies are achieving widespread use, they are profoundly affecting how the web works, and specifically how marketers can use it to leverage the variables of location, time, and social connectivity.

Many people here in the United States and within other technologically advanced nations are actually blind to the mobile revolution that is spreading across the globe. This became apparent to me this past year while on a vacation in Playa del Carmen, Mexico, a town that attracts tourists from all over the world, and that also has a vibrant local population.

Despite Mexico's status as a developing country, and one that most people would not consider a leader in technology, Wi-Fi availability in this little village was both common and expected by tourists and locals alike. In fact, after being seated at restaurants, almost without exception we were offered the password to use the establishment's Wi-Fi, and this even included restaurants that served as few as four tables.

The relevance of this trend occurred to me one day while I was sitting in the resort lobby. Other guests tended to congregate in this space due to the strength of the Wi-Fi signal and, also, I presume, because this open environment was designed for social interaction. One of the concierges that we have known for years stopped by to say hello, and during our conversation she asked a question that struck me as odd. She was curious about the cost of my Apple MacBook Pro.

Puzzled at first, I soon realized that of the dozens of computing devices being used by both guests and staff in that lobby, the only laptop was the one in front of me. It was out of place—a business device that belonged more in an office than in a predominantly social setting. I was indeed using it to work, checking on e-mails and keeping up with my blogging. And when I was finished with my work, I stowed it away in our room, bringing my mobile device with me before heading into town.

This town's main industry is tourism, and that means they must cater to visitors and merchants who are often on the go. Therefore, their communication devices have to be mobile. A desktop or laptop computer would be useless to most of them, which explains why they would not have an idea of how much one costs. The other reason is that mobile devices are most likely the first computers that many of the local residents in this developing country will own.

In a location where computing devices are largely mobile, they become part of the culture; they're used universally as tools for both professional and personal use, and for consumers and businesses alike. That kind of mainstream adoption creates amazing opportunities for connectivity and sharing that may not be evident to those of us who are frequently tied to our desktop and laptop computers purely out of habit.

It is inevitable that the majority of computing devices worldwide will be mobile. In fact, Apple's combined sales of iPhones and iPads already exceed all of their desktop and laptop computers by more than 400 percent—and moving even more in that direction. The challenge for businesses is to capitalize on this mobile attention, and to understand the full effect of its influence, which is much more than simple mobility—especially when a global audience is involved.

MOBILE MEANS BUSINESS

Mobile devices are becoming less expensive and more powerful, thereby raising the odds that many people will own more than one, with some dedicated to specific tasks—tools matched to a particular job. It's also possible that many of us will have just one device. As mobile phones get lighter and more powerful, and tablets get smaller, it's conceivable that many people will prefer to simplify their lives and use just one mobile device for both business and personal applications.

Businesses today need to understand why and how the intersection of mobile, local, and social is a marketing sweetspot, and how it is blurring the lines of time and space like a real-life Star Trek experience. Instead of investing a great deal of time learning the complexities of this rapidly changing technology, it's best to focus your energies on exploring ideal scenarios for using it to connect with your customers and their influencers. Then, investigate how you can make those scenarios reality.

For example: What if your business could instantly send a message to every individual within a given radius that is searching the web for a business like yours at a given moment? What message would you send? What would you like to know about them—and what would you like them to know about you and your business? Asking these questions is a healthy exercise, because when it comes to mobile marketing and the possibilities for using it to achieve greater connectivity and engagement, the question is not so much what is possible, but when.

There are many aspects of mobile that will delight those who love surprises, and that will give pause to those who believe the capabilities for tracking human behaviors have already gone too far. Regardless, the intersection of social, local, and mobile is becoming seamless to our daily activities. You may have heard the expression that in order to get new customers, you need to meet them where they are. This is the magic of mobile technologies—now you can, wherever and whenever they are.

MOBILE IS ATTENTION

It's easy to think of mobile as convenience, and it is. However, more important is that it has the attention of people who are never without their mobile devices. The more powerful these mobile devices become, and the more integral they are to our everyday lives, the greater the shift in consumer behaviors, and the marketing opportunities associated with them.

Think of mobile as the possibility that removes boundaries and limitations to create whatever your business can imagine. While this may seem far-fetched, you will soon learn that it is nonetheless true. Remember that old technology known as the facsimile, or fax machine, that could literally take the physical manifestation of ideas and instantaneously recreate them within seconds across multiple time zones? Take away the paper and telephone landlines, and you start to develop a sense of where this is going.

Consider the fact that mobile technologies now allow us to locate a new restaurant in real time, access guided instructions for easily locating it, be welcomed by name by the proprietor, and learn about recommendations that our friends may have left behind, while also discovering whether we know anyone who is presently dining there. You can accomplish all of this with the rapidly growing Foursquare service that is becoming a viable "location search engine" for local businesses, a category of search that Google and Facebook are also aggressively pursuing.

Mobile technologies work to jointly create better experiences for consumers—and the businesses embracing the technology use it to engage with their communities. In addition to reconnecting with regular customers, mobile works exceptionally well for reaching out to those passing through a particular location—something that local businesses should highly value. While location has always been vital to small business success, the intersection of mobile with social media is redefining the concept of local for businesses that do not even have a physical location.

Mobile gives people the power and the freedom to achieve their own solutions by allowing them to co-create with collaborative business marketers. Businesses need to study mobile behaviors and trends to learn what their customers value. This could range from daily specials, discounts on services, notifications about sales or contests, or simply a thank you or occasional gift for being a frequent customer. It is less about what businesses are offering and more about what consumers are expecting.

Mobile is more than a trend; it's a transformative shift that is well underway. Already over 50 percent of all local web searches are accomplished with mobile devices. And among others,

Facebook has announced they are going all in on mobile. Their Chief Technology Officer recently stated that within the next couple of years, nearly every one of Facebook's thousands of employees will be working on some aspect of mobile.

HOW IS YOUR BUSINESS ADAPTING TO MOBILE?

One of the reasons Facebook is embracing mobile is that they recognize it as the next frontier for social interaction. Mobile is inherently social because—notwithstanding the technology that digitally connects us—true socialization happens in person. Our physical social interactions are simply that much more enhanced when we can concurrently share them with our virtual communities. It's as if they are there with us. That capability that blurs the lines between physical and virtual reality is not something that will happen sitting alone in the office behind a desktop or laptop computer.

Not long after Facebook made the statement about embracing mobile, they also admitted that they were having challenges implementing it. Facebook and other companies were caught off guard by the mobile revolution, which is not surprising when you consider the first truly viable mainstream tablet computer, the iPad, was only introduced in early 2010.

Thus, to stay ahead of the game in your industry, your business needs to be asking how mobile could transform it. In regards to the interaction buyers have with your business, two important considerations are:

1. How will their location affect their interaction?
2. How will their social engagement at any given time influence their interaction?

MERGING THE VIRTUAL AND PHYSICAL WORLDS

Mobile promises to integrate digital content with what we experience every day, effectively merging the virtual world with physical reality. The mobile triggers responsible for making this integration faster and more seamless are QR or Quick Response codes. If you are not familiar with QR and other two-dimensional codes, they are similar to the barcodes used by retailers to track inventory and price products at the point of sale.

The key difference is that linear, one-dimensional barcodes only hold about 20 numerical digits of data, whereas QR (and other 2D codes such as Microsoft's MS tags) can hold approximately 7,000 alphanumeric characters of information. This capability—and the fact that the QR code technology is both free and open source—creates practically unlimited opportunities for their use as digital marketing triggers.

All QR codes are free and easy to generate using online code generators, such as the Microsoft Tag Manager (generates QR codes and MS tags), or native apps on mobile devices, such as Qrafter and i-Nigma. You can then capture the data within these codes with a code reader, sometimes referred to as a scanner, which works on most camera-enabled mobile devices. The readers are mostly free, with special features incurring incidental charges. Not all readers work with every type of mobile device, so search the web for one that is compatible with yours.

When using QR codes it is essential for businesses to initially focus less on the technology and more on how it can be best used to accomplish specific objectives. After that, be sure to test your codes on multiple mobile devices and in all types of potential environmental conditions that your audience may encounter.

One of the more common applications for using a QR code is to connect with online video that profiles some relevant aspect of the business. A local retailer could do this to capture how the personal touch of the in-store experience is superior to buying online. If you have experienced an Apple store during peak times, especially during the holidays, you know there is always an electric energy that could easily be captured on video to encourage more buyers to stop by.

Following are some ideas for how you can apply this to your business.

PRACTICAL USES OF QR CODES FOR BUSINESS

Here are some suggested ways to use QR codes that are already in practice by mainstream small businesses. Use these as ideas to develop applications that are especially appropriate to your business and the unique buying habits of your customers.

Where You Can Use QR Codes

- The back (or front and back) of your business card, or as a unique information card (See Figure 7.1.)
- Brochures and other marketing materials
- Direct mail pieces
- Event nametags, kiosks, and booths
- Company trucks, trailers, and store windows
- Billboards
- Point-of-sale

What QR Codes Can Link To

- Procedure for hiring your professional services
- Video introduction to your business
- Download your mobile app
- Connect with your LinkedIn or Facebook page

For patients by patients

www.StopAfib.org

 Why visit **StopAfib**.org?

- Learn what afib patients need to know
- Understand afib treatment options
- Read the latest atrial fibrillation news
- Watch video interviews with doctors
- Find afib patient services and resources
- Talk with others in forums & blogs

SCAN THIS QR CODE WITH YOUR SMART PHONE!

StopAfib.org — For Patients By Patients
HON Code Certified by *Health on the Net Foundation*

Figure 7.1   Patient card with QR code that links to important atrial fibrillation resources (Go to the Appendix for the complete story and links to related articles.)

- Special offers and discount coupons
- Digital surveys and customer feedback
- Enter a contest

There may be no limit to how QR codes and emerging technologies can be used to successfully capitalize on mobile, provided that you're able to manage consumer expectations. This may involve educating your customers about QR codes, and always providing value for them to engage with these mobile triggers.

MOBILE CLOUD COMPUTING

Looking down the road, we can see there are a number of emerging technologies that are all designed to make mobile commerce easier, faster, and more secure. To ignore mobile today is to avoid the imminent and obvious. People are mobile, they are social, and your business is most probably local in some way.

The technology that is dramatically enhancing and extending the capabilities of mobile is cloud computing. It is no longer necessary to carry a computer with a massive hard drive when you can store everything in the cloud, instantly access it, and share it across multiple desktop or laptop computers and mobile devices.

Services such as Dropbox.com give you access to literally every single document on your desktop computer through their mobile app. Thus, the changes you make to a document at your home office are instantly available from the field.

So how does this apply to you and your business? Well, odds are that you invest a great deal of effort into creating standardized company procedures. Yet you and your employees might only use some periodically, which introduces the risk of forgetting or skipping important steps when they are used—thereby resulting in costly mistakes.

Consider the advantages of creating instructional videos for all of your key operations, and having them readily accessible from any mobile device with QR codes that are neatly organized within a printed or digital pocket guide. You and your employees could retrieve videos for standard operating procedures from a smartphone when and where they are needed most. These could range from safety procedures to emergency repairs—all available right at your fingertips at all times.

MOBILE RESPONSIVE WEBSITES

More and more consumers are going to expect your website to be mobile-friendly. This will mean having larger buttons, click-to-call capabilities, and readily available directions. There are a number of ways to accomplish this, including a mobile-friendly Wordpress site or a redirect to a mobile site that is distinct from your primary website.

To keep everything simple, you should consider what is emerging as the option of choice, and that is building what is known as a mobile responsive site—something web developers can easily accomplish using mobile responsive Wordpress themes. A mobile responsive site automatically adjusts to the particular device being used to access your website. So, you only have one site to manage; however, it will adjust from a full display on a desktop or laptop screen to the progressively smaller screens of tablets and mobile phones. This will get and keep you current for the foreseeable future with the majority of devices that will continue to change as technologies and trends evolve.

LOCAL IS CONTEXT

The geolocation feature of mobile devices and computers gives marketers the capability to meet their customers where they are. Conversely, consumers are able to locate what they are most interested in—specifically, the people and businesses near their immediate location.

As more searches for local businesses are performed from a mobile device, adapting to mobile will be vital to the future success of any business, regardless of size. This mobile revolution is not being driven by businesses, but by the consumers that are embracing the wonders of mobile. Unfortunately, many businesses are not yet ready for this trend that is already sweeping across developing parts of the world.

Quantum physics tells us that we can define anything using two variables—space and time, a phenomenon that was featured in the popular film *Back to the Future* as the "space-time continuum." For instance, one minute from now you are still the same person occupying the same space as you are at this moment, with the exception that you will just be a little bit older. Incorporating the elements of time and location (location representing spatial objects such as physical businesses) into your marketing helps you to make it more accurate and better targeted to your buyers. It allows you to then focus your mobile marketing to *when* and *where* you expect your customers to be in the future.

That might sound a bit complicated, so let's look at an example. Consider the fact that most consumers use their mobile devices during the early morning and later afternoon and evening hours. This affects the specific times when businesses should be targeting them. So, you should ideally schedule your blog articles, social media posts, and newsletters to be delivered at points in time during the day and week when your audience is most receptive to consuming them—such as early in the week when they are fresh from the weekend. You may wish to consider publishing on Sunday if you market globally, since this engages with those getting a jump on the week while also bridging different time zones.

You can see how location and time are inextricably linked. Time determines location, because people often are where they are due to the time of the day, week, or even year—at home versus the office, in town versus on vacation, in their cars versus taking public transportation, and so forth. You know this to be fairly predictable if you are a local business, because we are all creatures of habit. So, the smart thing is to focus on the time to reach those in your community who you expect to be in proximity to your location.

Forget about mobile technologies for a minute, and simply ask yourself how time affects your business. When are people likely to need you most? For instance, when I was operating my seasonal landscape business I knew that customer demand was highest early Monday morning. That's when we were called upon most frequently to take care of issues that may have occurred over the weekend, such as a broken sprinkler head or fallen tree. It's also when our customers began preparing for a special event or holiday weekend, thereby giving us notice of any special enhancements or extra attention to detail that was necessary for their property.

How about your business? If you are a hair stylist you are certainly going to be busy before prom, Mother's Day, and most holidays, especially on weekends. There is a rhythm to every business, one that defines the day, week, season, and year. Mobile technologies are going to amplify that in many ways, probably by stretching peak times of activity. It's up to businesses to determine how to respond to the respective changes.

You too will personally make decisions that will differ based upon your location. For example, aren't you more likely to splurge on a purchase while on a personal vacation than when on a business trip? In your local and familiar environment you know where to find the best bargains, and therefore tend to take advantage of them. Is it possible for marketing to pull you out of those patterns? Indeed it is—when it finds you based on your location, and in real time. This is why Facebook and so many others are fully committed to making their businesses mobile-friendly—and why your business should do the same.

After working with golf course owners and managers I discovered their challenges were quite varied, with location being a key factor. Some golf courses, especially resorts, are considered to be destination courses, whereas many public golf courses are located within close proximity to their frequent customers. Women's groups favored weekdays for play at local courses while men actively sought out the premium times at destination courses on weekends. Thus the make-up of the group affects when they play, and most likely affects which golf course they choose as well.

What is essential for businesses is to always be studying the patterned behaviors of its customers. Remember, it is more important to be aware of how social media is changing consumer behaviors than to necessarily be using it. The same holds true for mobile.

THE CONTEXT OF TIME AND PLACE

When it comes to business marketing, there is an important distinction to make between local and location. Local businesses have a distinct advantage due to their physical location—proximity to a population of potential buyers.

Yet, every business can capitalize on local because, in addition to location, it is affected by a number of influences including consumer interests, social behaviors, and all types of human interactions.

How these influences intersect creates a number of ways to interpret local contexts. And you can use any one of these— or a combination of several—to create distinct advantages for your business. Location marketing rightfully capitalizes on one component—proximity—that translates into convenience and, therefore, saving the customer time. You can charge more for convenience or not; but whatever you decide, you should incorporate it into your marketing plans to accomplish specific business objectives. Time is a valuable commodity that you can effectively use to be more local to the markets you serve. The only challenge is building a business model to uniquely capitalize on it.

For example, the Internet enabled non-local businesses to effectively become local: Amazon, Zappos, and Warby Parker are just a few that have used different business models to benefit from consumer desires for convenience and saving time. You can get products shipped to you within a day or two from Amazon and pay little or no premium for the benefit. That's convenient. Zappos allows you to purchase shoes and other products, while providing a full year to return them for a refund—and shipping is free both ways.

And the Warby Parker website allows you to virtually "try on" eyewear frames from your computer by simply uploading your photo. After narrowing down your choices, they will send you up to five frames at a time to physically examine for five days, with free shipping both ways. (Hmm, I wonder where they got that idea?) After that, you place your order online.

Small businesspeople in my live audiences at events often ask for examples from their industry. Often, there aren't any. Warby Parker may well have borrowed Zappos' idea with respect to free trials. They may also have taken a cue from TOMS Shoes (discussed in Chapter 4) by choosing to give away one pair of eyeglasses to the underprivileged for every pair they sell. Thus, while not even being in the shoe business, Warby Parker seems to have borrowed concepts from that industry that are significant aspects of their business model. A lack of industry-specific examples simply means that your business can be the one that leads it by improvising and adapting from proven methods used successfully in other industries—while then serving as a future example for others.

TAKE YOUR AUDIENCE ON A JOURNEY

There is a difference between television and live, on-location television. Live television comes alive because there is anticipation and excitement about what is going to happen next. Mobile technologies now make it possible to bring those kinds of experiential feelings to your customers.

Photographer John Butterill applied this principle to Google+ Hangouts by taking it mobile—and indeed there is an equally significant, if not remarkable difference. A Google+ hangout is a live video conference using the free Google+ platform and it is proving to be a source of new possibilities for innovative small businesses. To watch the YouTube video, go to the Appendix for the link; it shows how John and his friends used Hangout to take his audience on a live virtual ride through nature. John dramatically enhanced mobile's value by combining it with a Google+ hangout; he also engaged his professional community, who enthusiastically joined him on that ride.

You don't have to go into the wilderness as John did to wow your audience, but just imagine gathering some of your best customers together to collaborate live and on-location to share new ideas that everyone could then benefit from. While you can of course accomplish that in an office environment, perhaps you could choose one that is more inviting. You could also do this to interact with customers or guests who are with you in person to bring them together with others who are live on Google+.

This could prove especially interesting for any business that operates from an interesting environment—the hospitality industry being just one example. So, if you are a destination resort you could schedule a Google+ hangout so that your customers around the country or the world could experience a sunset or a view of the mountains while sharing a conversation with you at your location, thereby subtly reminding them that it may be time for a return visit.

SOCIAL IS INFLUENCE

The most independent among us have to admit that others influence our behavior. It's also an undeniable fact that location affects behavior. Put someone in a favorable environment and their behavior will usually improve. This was actually proven in a well-known factory study in which worker productivity improved when the lighting was enhanced. Interestingly, behavior also improved when the lighting was reduced. Why?

The assumption that has been debated at length—but is nonetheless plausible—is that people assume you care when they know you are watching—and are more likely to perform better as a result. It is true that as children, most of us learned to show off when we knew our parents were watching. So, businesses that want to encourage specific consumer actions will want to learn more about the social dynamics in their communities—specifically, who influences whom. This is fairly easy to do if you happen to be Facebook friends—and is just one more reason to be better connected.

It's therefore not surprising that social influence is a topic that interests many businesses these days. Klout.com is a controversial service that calculates a numerical score that theoretically represents your social influence by measuring a number of variables on various social networks, including the most obvious—do people respond to your comments and tweets? If so, how many and who are they, and do they further influence others? While the jury is still out on Klout's accuracy and relevance, the truth is that we are all influenced by others, and that, of course, is the basis for celebrity endorsements.

When a business hangs its hat on the reputation of a celebrity, it attempts to create alignment with the fans and followers the celebrity influences. Who influences you? It may be your family, close friends, and your work associates, many of whom you are connected with through the social networks. This social context is not only of interest to Klout, but to Facebook, Google, and many other businesses that recognize social context as integral to the future of search.

Thus, the power of mobile is to not only engage consumers, but their influencers as well. This is why the many applications on Facebook want to access all of your information. They want to not only connect with you, but with all of your friends who presumably have some influence on your decision-making process, and you on theirs. The interconnected social graphs will tell that story.

So what does this mean for your business? It means that the opportunities lie in connecting to connections. By tapping into your social graphs, you can potentially reach new customers—as well as those who have an influence on them becoming or remaining a customer. Of course, this is only possible if you are using your networks to engage. As we learned in the previous chapter, more openness and transparency leads to more opportunities for connecting.

In the story about my client Bob from Chapter 2, it was noted we were willing to do anything possible to earn his trust and retain him as a loyal client. So, when we were preparing our proposal we also reached out to mutual friends to learn everything we could about the factors that might influence his decision. You can now accomplish this digitally by studying the people with whom your customers are sharing on their social channels, and then connecting the dots further to their influencers. This is not an exact science, by any means, but it can nevertheless provide valuable insights for making better business decisions.

There are quite a few social search engines you can use for this purpose; SocialMention.com, Topsy.com, and Wajam.com being a few. And always keep in mind that information is only that—information. You still have to make decisions about specifically how to put it to good use.

SOCIAL CREATES ALIGNMENT

Social marketing is a process of strategically and progressively creating alignment with your ideal customers. It's a way to draw them in closer, first by using valuable content marketing information that solidifies your credibility. Then, you have to make emotional connections to convert that attention and engagement into new business. This is the power of social, and why it is more important to be better connected to build deeper social alignment.

Alignment is the product of countless contextual social factors that influence behaviors. On a practical business level, you can tap into the value of social context by building a profile of your customers' influences, either individually or by grouping them according to similar behaviors.

Here are some factors to consider.

- **Interests.** We are all inherently attracted to those who share our interests. This is evident from the conversations on Facebook and other social networks, and one reason why you should connect the dots to learn more about your connections. You can literally do this by studying your LinkedIn InMaps. (Go to the Appendix for the link to an informative YouTube video.)

- **Industry and Profession.** We spend the majority of our waking life at work, so our co-workers and industry colleagues naturally have a great deal of influence on us. These individuals are a great source of business referrals—something you can encourage more of by building your networks and occasionally asking for introductions.

- **Influencers.** There are people in every social circle that significantly influence the majority. You can use services such as Klout to measure this; however, if you are actively connecting and networking, you will learn this from the social signals within your networks.

YOUR MOBILE STRATEGY

Mobile marketing success starts with understanding your audience, then implementing an appropriate strategy to engage them, and ultimately delivering a favorable user experience. There are a number of factors to consider, the first of which is to understand what your audience needs and desires. Here are some sample ideas to consider.

Understand Your Target Audience

- Do they need instructions on how to connect with your business using mobile?
- Should they be using a specific type of mobile device to best access your information?
- Do you want them to activate geolocation to enable tracking?
- Will your QR codes be scanned indoors or outside, and from what distance?

Have Clear Objectives

- Are you trying to grow your e-mail list or build your social network (something we'll discuss at length in the next chapter)?

- Should you consider split testing—offering different incentives to measure the response rates for each?
- What is the expected outcome of your call to action, and does your offer clearly communicate it?

Provide Useful and Valuable Incentives

- Get VIP access to special events.
- Provide discounts on products and services.
- Enter a contest to win.

When planning your mobile marketing strategy you should consider every relevant variable, from before, during, and after you engage with your audience. While all of this may appear fairly simple, it's always best to be certain when technology and human behavior are involved. Even major brands have made embarrassing mistakes with QR code marketing campaigns because they overlooked minor details. Without mentioning specific examples, the common mistakes are displaying QR codes in subways or other locations where there is no Internet signal. However, notwithstanding that limitation, the better QR code readers will bookmark a page so that it can be accessed when you do have a signal.

There is a learning curve with mobile, but it's not a very complicated one. Start small, take your time, and adapt from what you notice is working. There may be some complexities associated with the technology, but actually using it isn't—if you take it one step at a time and stay focused on the big picture. It's all about creating user experiences that progressively build alignment between your business and your customers—all of which leads to favorable connections.

Try This: Design for Location and Time

To capitalize on the influences of social, local, and mobile, your business should design its marketing when and where you expect your customers to be in the future—in other words, for location and time.

Where is the Location of your future customers.

- Where are your customers when you are open for business?
- Where are they likely to be active on social media?
- Where do they live and work?
- Where are they when using mobile devices—at home, work, or commuting?
- Where are their influencers—local or remote?

When is the Time your future customers are buying.

- When are your customers most likely to call your business?
- When are they most likely to be near your location?
- When are they most likely to be using their mobile devices?
- When are they most likely to be receptive to an e-mail?
- When are they checking their social media accounts?

While you may not have the answers right away, some study and investigation will give you a better idea of the behaviors of your customers. Use your results to start building your mobile marketing strategy.

CHAPTER 8

Creating Digital Marketing Assets

Building digital marketing assets that yield sustainable business value ensures the future success of your business.

In the days before the Internet, the primary marketing vehicle for many small businesses was the Yellow Pages, an advertising section within local community telephone directories. In many ways, it was what their website would be today. The investment in phone book advertising had to be renewed periodically when new books were printed, but for the better part of the year, the business owned a piece of real estate in the go-to source for finding local businesses.

Yellow Page advertising was a turnkey arrangement designed especially for small businesses. The phone company made the arrangement attractive by taking care of the details—including the distribution of those books into thousands of homes—where they were usually within reach of the telephone. Of course, back then telephones were attached to wiring within the walls, making them immobile. So, in a sense, Yellow Page advertising was the location marketing of the time, because those books were always close by the telephone. In terms of consumer habits, there was no better place to be highly visible.

Telephone books had some staying power because homeowners and businesses often retained copies that included their personal notations. However, the true durable asset was not the books, but the list of customers to whom those books were delivered, which the phone company owned.

From the first day residents and businesses had their phone lines connected, they implicitly granted permission to the phone company to receive an ongoing stream of phone books. In that regard, Yellow Page advertising was what we now call permission marketing, a term popularized by marketing expert and author Seth Godin. Every home and business with a telephone automatically received phone books that were part useful content (telephone numbers and addresses) and part advertising. In fact, many people even looked forward to receiving them because it was their source of connectivity to the local community. This was music to the ears of the businesses that paid dearly to be profiled on those pages.

An example of permission marketing today is e-mail marketing, at least when legitimate opt-in permission practices are followed. If you are building your e-mail list, you are building a digital marketing asset—something you're also doing when you acquire subscribers to your blog. There are significant differences between the two in terms of ownership and control, but they are assets that your business owns and should be valued for their ability to reach out to your audience and convert their attention into new business.

Today you have many ways to digitally connect with your customers; most essential is designing, building, and securing digital marketing assets that you own, so that you will always be in control of your business destiny.

CONTENT IS ALWAYS AN ASSET

As you know from the Introduction, even before the Internet, content marketing was a viable alternative to Yellow Page advertising— it was simply accomplished in print form. In my previous business, I wrote content in the form of newsworthy articles for the local newspapers, and we were fortunate to have several in our suburban Chicago community. A primary concern was to focus on providing useful information without being too self-promotional, otherwise the articles I wrote would not be published.

This is equally true today, except that now that we have Facebook pages, blogs, and Twitter. Everyone is a publisher today, and the cardinal rule of creating useful content is easily forgotten. Take this to heart, because if you spam your communities they will disconnect from the marketing assets you are working hard to build.

We were delighted with any coverage in the local newspapers because people responded to them like nothing else. In the days before Facebook, the Internet, and e-mail, the local paper was the most credible source of news in nearly every community. As a result, we easily distinguished our business as a trusted community and industry leader. Your business blog can now accomplish the same if you make blogging a regular practice.

We took the steps to create physical assets of those published newspaper articles by making thousands of reprints to distribute to potential buyers in order to establish our expertise and credibility. We always kept a ready supply of pocket folders that contained a one-page sheet that detailed our company capabilities and service offerings. We packed that folder with dozens of news articles profiling our community stewardship, recent awards, and human-interest stories. This is something you can now accomplish digitally by aggregating blog links and adding durable content to create a complete package.

There are challenges associated with this form of marketing that are just as relevant today as they were back then, which explains why it worked so well for us; namely, that other companies were not willing to make the effort. The practice of content marketing requires work—and also some ingenuity. In addition to creating the content, we also had to learn how to get past the media gatekeepers, which is also relevant today in terms of getting access to influential bloggers to build your platform.

Some of the challenges we experienced, which are similar to what you may encounter today, are as follows:

- *We Had No Ownership.* The print media outlets owned and managed everything, and usually made it clear they didn't necessarily care about our perspectives—just our content, which they then owned after we gave it to them. It was all just part of the game.

- *We Had No Control.* Our messages were often compromised because they had to be filtered by a journalist who didn't know much about our business, and was probably more focused only on fitting the content to the page.

- *It Was a Gated Process.* Though it changed over time, there was a period when getting the attention of the local newspaper editor was like getting an appointment with the Wizard of Oz: "No one gets in to see the Wizard. Not no one; not no how!"

- *It Was Time-Sensitive.* To ensure the relevancy of our article reprints, we chose to use only those that had been published within the past year or so. Imagine that? The same year was considered relevant back then. So, we had to work our magic to make sure we achieved two or three good published articles each year that had sustainable value.

- *We Had Limited Bandwidth.* Even when we had plenty of relevant news to share, it was essential to time our submissions to avoid the risk of bothering the editors and getting cut off completely.

Despite the challenges, there was one memorable success you may want to consider that worked exceptionally well—and that is to not underestimate the value of an appropriate gift, something my friend Michael Stelzner discusses in detail in his book, *Launch: How to Quickly Propel Your Business Beyond the Competition* (Wiley, 2011).

Since our company was in the business of enhancing nature, it seemed appropriate to include a live plant while hand-delivering a particular news release—a process that consumed an entire day. One editor refused it because it was against policy for her to accept gifts. I suggested that it was just something to brighten up the entire office for everyone.

I'm not sure what happened to that plant, but that paper not only published my article, they did two follow-up feature stories. And the others followed suit. That investment of time and four or five plants resulted in a total of 11 articles being published about our business. Traditional media was so powerful back then that I would have invested a week of my time had I expected those kinds of results.

Today you and your business are the media, and you can achieve amazing results from your content marketing, too. However, just as I learned nearly twenty years ago, your results will range from challenging to amazing. All you can do is make this a practice and learn as you build your marketing assets.

DIGITAL CONTENT MARKETING ASSETS

A basic definition of a business asset is anything from which the company can derive value, either from its outright sale or use in the business operations. So, monetary instruments such as stocks, bonds, and inventory that can be sold for cash are considered assets. When you sell a business, you quickly discover where its true value lies; that is, anything that can easily be converted into cash or reliably produce future revenue streams. This includes signed contracts, e-mail lists, and other digital properties that will readily connect the new owner with your customers and online communities.

Hard assets used to be the power play in business, but this is no longer the case in this recessionary economy where abundant supply and competition have depressed pricing. These days the sustainable value in businesses is within customer lists and any subscription assets such as a blog or e-mail newsletter. Now that everyone has the ability to take control of their media, those with the skills for harnessing its potential have a distinct advantage in that they can control their business destiny. Though you may someday plan to sell your business, you're probably more interested in building these assets to contribute to its profitability and growth, both now and for the foreseeable future.

While any digital property that represents your business holds value, we will focus on the three most essential—your website, blog, and e-mail marketing newsletters. All of these vehicles have the potential for converting engagement into profitable outcomes for as long as you own and care for them. They all have unlimited upside potential. This is one reason why many top bloggers have turned down lucrative offers to sell their blogs—because they have no idea what the future upside potential may be, other than the fact that it will be greater than it is today.

In considering only digital properties that you own, we are effectively excluding your presence on all social networking sites. This is not meant to diminish their value, but to underscore the fact that you have no control over them and therefore are subject to any number of changes that could occur, including modifications of the terms and conditions, their sale, or being shut down altogether.

As a point of clarity, you obviously do not own your customers; however, you do own the access they have provided you. That's what makes them permission marketing assets. This is why you need to give the access they have granted you your utmost respect. Sadly, the amount of e-mail spam we all receive suggests that many businesses do not quite grasp this concept.

WEBSITES, BLOGS, AND E-MAIL NEWSLETTERS—THE THREE ESSENTIAL DIGITAL BUSINESS ASSETS

A website has traditionally been the primary Internet marketing asset for businesses. However, the maturation and growth of blogging is changing that. The reason for this is that the relevant information Google is hungry for is more likely to be found on blogs. One example of this is the Huffington Post, a mega blog which AOL media purchased for over $300 million, primarily for the opportunity to advertise to the millions of active readers and subscribers that keep coming back for fresh and relevant content.

While you may not be planning to advertise on your blog, you nevertheless should be interested in building a growing community to earn their permission for periodically making product and service offers. Copyblogger.com and SocialMediaExaminer.com are two extraordinarily successful business blogs that do this well—Copyblogger sells a suite of software products and the Social Media Examiner sells training and events. Unlike the more traditional advertising model for monetizing blogs, their respective approaches of using content to build a defined audience and developing products and services especially for them, is one that can be successfully adapted to many small businesses.

BLOGS VERSUS WEBSITES—THE REAL DIFFERENCE

Most people think of a website as a digital storefront—a place for offering products and services and other commercial activities that you can also accomplish with a blog. So then, you may wonder, what exactly is the difference between a blog and a website?

Blogs and websites are both considered websites, with the former being interactive and the latter predominantly static or inactive. That's one important distinction.

If consumers are ready to buy, and are therefore primarily interested in product details such as specifications and pricing, then a traditional website is the ideal means for converting that interest into profitable sales. Whereas if those consumers are doing research and otherwise taking the time to educate themselves, a blog is going to be more likely to hold their attention.

The most promising option for most businesses today is a hybrid site that combines the best of both, and it's a matter of knowing your customer to determine which is best for your business. Buyers need to know what you are selling because that tells them more about how you can help them. You can profile that front and center on the home page of your site, in the sidebar, or on a secondary page.

However, most important is to not think of your blog as something that sits on your website. This compromises its value. Instead, consider it for what it is—a source of valuable information that attracts and educates interested buyers and holds their attention, while also providing significant SEO benefits. Now consider if that should be primary or secondary to the home page of your site.

ADVANTAGES OF A BLOG AS YOUR SOCIAL MEDIA HUB

- **Ownership.** You own your blog content for life when its online address is a unique URL that you own. This allows you to even switch blogging platforms and take all of your content, comments, and valuable links with you.

- **Flexibility.** There is more functionality possible on a blog than most people will ever need. Wordpress plugins make it especially easy for anyone to add and remove features.

- **Content Management.** A search feature on your blog allows visitors to find just what they are looking for from hundreds or thousands of blog posts. You can and should also use it to link back to your previous work to further engage your reader.

- **Community.** A personalized blog becomes a destination that you inhabit, and that helps to humanize your business to make it more attractive to your community.

- **Multi-Media.** You can host audio, video, images, and other forms of content on your blog to keep your audience more engaged.

- **Sharing.** Readers can easily share your blog posts with friends to extend your message and introduce you to new communities.

- **Expertise.** When you blog on a regular basis you develop new perspectives that liberate your expertise.

- **E-mail Capture.** You can capture e-mail addresses on your blog to build your list.

- **Reputation Management.** Google acknowledges blogs as respected sources of news. As such, your blog is a representation of your accumulated experience as a professional in your industry.

- **Control.** Unlike most social media networks, you have complete control over your blog. You determine the culture, functionality, and overall look and feel.

Blogs were distinct from traditional websites in their early days. Now they are seamlessly working together as one—serving up informational content along with offerings of products, services, and advertising. They also easily integrate with your social media channels and digital newsletters—both of which also combine well with each other. For more on getting started with and getting better at blogging, go to the online resources in the Appendix.

THE ART OF E-MAIL MARKETING

For the most part, there are two types of e-mail marketing newsletters—those that we eagerly anticipate because they have developed a special relationship with us—and those that waste our time or outright annoy us. The art of e-mail marketing starts by honoring the fact that your subscriber respects your business enough to give you direct access to their inbox.

Your blog serves as a source of content for building and retaining an audience, and your social media channels serve to engage them further, but the most powerful tool for directly converting that interest and engagement into sales is your e-mail marketing. This is accomplished by using it to provide value and a special feeling of community, even intimacy.

There are newsletters (most are digital these days) that have been regularly published since the 1960s, for which loyal subscribers pay annual rates in the hundreds of dollars because the quality of the information is consistently valuable and worth it. While it is not likely that your subscribers are paying for your newsletter, you may want to consider treating it as if they are in order to build a fanatically loyal subscriber base that is truly an enviable asset.

Paid newsletters have to deliver or they lose subscribers—period. They can never miss a scheduled delivery, and the content has to be everything that the original offer promised. Consider rethinking your e-mail marketing from the standpoint of the promises that you will keep—no matter what. That's how you will build your list—and a tribe of fans that will respond to your occasional business offers because you have given them so much value in return.

MAKING THE MOST OF YOUR DIGITAL ASSETS

The healthiest approach you can take towards all of your digital marketing assets is to consider them works in progress—as they should be if they are growing. It takes work to build these assets, and they are never done. There is always more to do.

Thus, you should never aspire to create perfect sites and pages—just close enough. This gives you the freedom to easily adapt to the next trend that is just around the corner, such as mobile-responsive websites discussed in the previous chapter.

Your digital assets are the future of your business—the tribe of customers and influencers you have now and your ability to make connections to new ones. Other than your valued team members, what could be more important to the future success of your business than customers? This is why it's essential to consider them to be your new business partners, and that means getting to know them better.

KNOW YOUR AUDIENCE

Those of us who speak professionally go through a deliberate and intensive process for understanding the people to whom we're presenting before we set foot on the stage. Even if I've previously spoken to a particular group, I will take the time to interview audience members in advance to learn what is most relevant to them now. I want to determine what the hot issues are, and uncover anything else that may have changed since the last time I presented to them.

You can and should do this with your audience using your digital properties. Are you studying who is connecting to you? Most of the major social networks show you who your recent followers or subscribers are, and virtually every e-mail newsletter service will do the same. Do you take a moment every now and then to check out their profiles and send a few kind words?

The more specific you can be, the better. For example, this book is being written for mainstream and largely non-technical small businesses. Some people consider the definition of small business to be organizations with annual revenue of less than $500 million, whereas my definition is more like less than $50 million, and often even much less than that. You have to intimately know your audience so you can better understand and address their challenges and opportunities, and that will also be evident in subtle ways, such as the language you use.

The name of this game is access, and for your audience to give you that, they will want to know more about you. While bios and things of that nature are useful, the proof is truly in the content that you share. You will grow your communities by continuously earning their respect and trust—it works pretty much the same for every community.

ESTABLISH EXPECTATIONS

Whether you are building a community with your blog, e-mail marketing, or social media accounts, you want to set expectations that make it clear that you are a professional. I have a colleague who delivers a weekly newsletter every Sunday morning, without exception. In the several years since I've been a subscriber, he has not missed a single week. That kind of rare consistency is more than an expectation; it sends a strong message of professionalism to his community that earns their respect.

One of the standards I have for my blog and newsletter communities is I will never share anything with which I have not had direct experience, which means either I use—or would considering using—everything I recommend. There is enormous value in helping your communities limit the number of choices available for solving their problems. If they trust you, they want your personal opinion, and they will value and respect your leadership to eliminate a product or service that is not right for them. Taking a stand for the benefit of your community is a signature practice that I learned from my friend Chris Brogan, who has built his reputation on trust and an uncompromising commitment to his communities.

Of course, be sure your community knows that you are indeed a business, and will therefore offer them products from time to time. While many businesses use their digital assets to do too much selling, some surprisingly don't do enough. Remember—your community considers your products and services to be souvenirs. Set expectations to announce an upcoming offer in advance, preferably more than once. Then when the time comes, take the opportunity you've earned to promote its value and benefits for them—in a professional manner, of course.

KEEP RAISING THE BAR

Assets appreciate if you invest in them. If you make sensible improvements to your home, for example, you will more than likely get a return on that investment in the form of a higher price or faster sale when you decide to sell it. You have to take good care of your digital marketing assets in a similar way: by caring for the community, answering their comments, publishing valuable content, and making improvements to keep pace with changing needs, consumer trends, and advances in technologies.

Raising the bar for your audience usually means raising it for you and your business as well—because when a business stops growing, it starts to die. Change is happening every single day. The challenge is being tuned into your markets well enough to discern these changes, and then contributing to shaping favorable change. In community-driven markets customers lead changes. Community-driven markets are those in which information makes a difference in buying decisions. This includes most service industries.

Your business should also be using your social channels to get honest feedback from customers. One of the best methods for discerning customer expectations is asking good questions and noticing patterns. People will all eventually speak the truth when given the opportunity to speak freely—and without risk.

A good question to ask is, "Do you think others would say we provide good value?" How *they* personally feel will then follow, and that will give your business clues about the changes they are expecting.

Other good questions are the ones that nobody else is asking them. Such as: "Would you pay more for a better product?" A favorable reply may suggest your quality is not where it needs to be, and that your customer is willing to pay more for what they really want.

Once again, it's helpful to look for market and industry trends and study the changes you are noticing. You can search Alltop.com and Technorati.com for popular blogs and websites that are specifically related to your industry or profession. My recommendation is to subscribe to some of the top blogs in your industry using Google Reader—which allows you to easily consume an enormous amount of online content by subscribing to the RSS feeds of the blogs. (Go to the Appendix for more on using Google Reader.)

After learning how to use the Google Reader, you may find it easier to consume the content on your mobile device using a feature-rich app. One I highly recommend for the iPad that instantly merges with Google Reader and serves up the content in a user-friendly manner is Mr. Reader. This tool lets you organize and prioritize the feeds, and then easily share them on the social networks or save them to apps such as Pocket or Reader, which will synchronize it across all of your devices for reading later—wherever you are. Search for other RSS reader apps that are suited to your particular devices, with Reeder being one that works nicely with the iPhone.

SECURE YOUR ASSETS

Consider the following: If there was a cataclysmic Internet event, and you only had time to safeguard one of your online marketing assets, which one would it be and why? You should never have to worry about this if you are taking steps to consistently secure your content and associated communities. I use a service to back up my blog that sends me a file that I then save to my computer, as well as to the cloud. In addition to that, my hosting company is backing up their servers to multiple locations. I also have multiple Wordpress plugins (pieces of code) that are designed to protect my site from being hacked.

When you own an asset, you carry the burden for taking care of it. The trend is to use cloud backup capabilities that automatically do the work for you. The major social networks should already be accomplishing this more effectively than you can yourself. However, you still have the capability to personally download your connections from LinkedIn, and while clunky, even Facebook offers a service for downloading your content.

Always be thinking about your online marketing channels in terms of assets that you own. Odds are most of your Facebook friends are also connected with you on LinkedIn, and those connections are easily secured. Of course, having multiple copies of your e-mail newsletter list and the content from your blog and website is not only essential, it will give you the peace of mind that comes from knowing you've secured your ability to generate future revenue.

The truth is none of us would want to lose any of our digital assets. The content that we have created should be secured at whatever cost is necessary, and the same goes for the communities and tribes that have formed around that content. Nothing is foolproof, so needless to say, it's wise to save all of your data in multiple locations using the methods and media that give you the most confidence. I've mentioned that I rely on Dropbox for the cloud, and have depended on Lacie for solid-state portable hard drives.

BE READY TO PIVOT

Technology start-ups are fond of using the word *pivot* to describe their nimble responsiveness to market and technological changes. They have to be prepared to pivot almost instantly in their fast-paced world to take advantage of market opportunities and ensure their survival—or achieve outrageous success. It's a mindset that every business should adopt, because the truth is we are all plugged into these technologies in a big way—or should be—due to the effects they have on the communities we serve.

I've made my share of mistakes in regards to social marketing; after all, that's how we learn. And I've also done a few things right. Being an early adopter and staying in the game has proved invaluable. Most valuable has been my dedication to making blogging a practice that is not subject to compromise. Most small businesses are not blogging, despite what many studies may suggest. That would change if they knew of the truly immeasurable personal and business benefits—and they will become evident soon enough, which is why I fully expect blogging and other forms of content and social marketing to go mainstream in the next couple of years.

When I made a major career pivot—selling my landscape business to focus exclusively on helping small businesses use social media and Internet marketing, I had two types of assets to sell: trucks, trailers, and other hard assets—and a highly ranked website and list of longtime and loyal clients. None of the buyers wanted my "iron," which fortunately I was able to unload to dealers and individuals with the help of eBay.

However, the two companies I entertained offers from both wanted to buy our contracts, customer lists, and websites. We were not a large company; however, we weren't all that small either, and we were well established within a specific community. As one of the potential buyers said in regards to his interest in our company, "I'm tired of driving around your community to get to my other customers." That is what it means to be hyperlocal—owning a trusted presence in a defined community, however large or small it may be.

The future value of your company demands that you dedicate yourself to building bankable marketing assets that you own. If you start now, or commit to doing more than you have been, you will look back, as I often do, and thank yourself. You will never regret the time you invest in this, and know that it's never too late to join this party.

Are you ready to pivot?

Try This: Build Digital Assets

The future of your business is dependent upon its ability to communicate quickly and effectively with its communities—including customers, influencers, and community friends.

All of the digital marketing assets discussed here scale—meaning, their growth potential is not limited by your efforts. You can build a community of a few dozen or hundreds of thousands with virtually the same effort. What is necessary is properly building, maintaining, and then securing your digital assets.

Considering the three essential content marketing assets: your website, blog, and e-mail newsletter:

1. What is your current state of readiness?

2. What are you doing to grow them?

3. What are you willing to commit to for the next year to start building your digital marketing assets?

- Take action on at least one item to get started or get better. A small community is better than none, because if you make any commitment at all to build and grow it—your efforts will be rewarded.

- If you cannot make a weekly commitment, then do it monthly. If not monthly, then make a quarterly commitment to blog, send a quality newsletter, or freshen the content on your website.

CHAPTER 9

Relationship Selling in the Trust Economy

The sales process is more than a series of steps. It is a guidance system that makes everyone aware of what should be happening and how to get on track if it isn't.

The process of social marketing should ultimately convert attention and engagement into profitable outcomes. That means there has to be a way to translate interaction into sales—and hopefully relationships that lead to repeat business and referrals.

This book assumes that your business derives the majority of its revenue—if not all of it—from the sale of tangible products or services. You don't necessarily accomplish this conversion digitally; rather, the process involves salespeople working with your customers or clients. To be clear, the one thing that stands between your social media engagement and cashing checks is the integration of basic selling principles into your social marketing process.

Despite what you may have heard about being a born salesperson, selling is a skill that can be developed with experience. It's easy enough to do when you apply the principles you have learned in this book—earning your audience's attention, engaging them, and then—once you have earned their trust—taking them to a better place with your products and services. As you know, you can accomplish this by making emotional connections with potential buyers, completing what legendary sales trainer Zig Ziglar describes as a "transference of feeling."

THE SALES PROCESS

The selling profession has the potential to be one of the most rewarding or frustrating, depending upon a variety of factors, such as ongoing training, experience, and day-to-day preparation. It may seem surprising, but far too many small businesses don't have a well-designed sales process that their people are trained to execute. And even if they do, it is not often written down—which means that their selling practices are not always consistent, thereby resulting in mistakes, lost opportunities, and unhappy customers.

What they often *do* have are competent salespeople who have learned how to earn the trust of buyers in order to consummate a sale. And one quality they usually share is a high level of organization. If you care about and are interested in people—and you understand what you are selling—you should do nicely in the profession of selling. But if you happen to be organized as well, you will achieve far more. This is one of the primary reasons to have a sales process in place: it delivers a more consistently favorable experience for each and every customer that walks through your doors, regardless of the salesperson's level of skill or experience.

When you combine good communication and presentation skills with a solid sales process to keep the salesperson organized and on track, your rate of closing sales will increase dramatically. This is because the sales process is more than a series of steps to follow; it is also a guidance system that makes everyone aware of what should be happening and how to get on track if it isn't.

You'll also discover that your sales process is a powerful marketing tool. It gives your buyers the confidence that you can solve their problems, and assures them that you aren't wasting their time or experimenting with their money as you do it. You will recall from the Introduction that when I entered the green industry, I discovered that every local land-scape company seemed to approach things differently. This not only included how they executed the work, but how they sold it as well.

While I experienced my share of early failures as an entrepreneur, one thing that served me well after 10 years of corporate sales and marketing was my dedication to writing down what happened after every selling situation. I used what I learned from those circumstances to produce a more favorable outcome the next time around. I take a similar approach in my current work by debriefing every single speaking engagement to learn how to refine and polish them for future audiences.

You may consider your sales process to be about selling the product that is ultimately delivered to the customer. But it is much more—encompassing everything that a customer experiences with your company, from before to long after the sale. In fact, what happens after the sale is vitally important, and is one of the many reasons why you must design your process around your customer. Your objective is to create the most delightful experience possible for each and every customer, regardless of who they are or which salesperson happens to be working with them.

While it's not always written down, I've found that most businesses do have a sales process—one that they've developed over the years to bring in new or recurring business. It's a process that the owner created as the original salesperson—one in which they naturally found their way and managed to replicate it over time.

That said, I would suggest every business take the time to write down the steps of their selling process. It is a surefire way to be more conscious of precisely what you need to do to get things done, and will prove to be useful for adding or eliminating steps to make the process better or cleaner. It will also prove invaluable for making a smooth transition as you add staff or reassign responsibilities.

A well-designed process organizes what is essential, thereby freeing the salesperson to focus on the customer. You'll discover that everyone has their way of relating to others—and when they are free to do that they will naturally make better decisions and the necessary emotional connections. But that only happens when they don't have to worry about what to do next.

YOUR FRONT-STAGE PROCESS

The only thing more frustrating than working with a company without a clearly defined process is working with one that cannot articulate it. This is often the case with technology companies, because they often assume everyone understands technology as they do.

One of the mistakes many of us make in selling situations is sharing too much information with the buyer, thereby confusing them and eventually losing both their confidence and the sale. If your marketing is effectively attracting interest and engagement but you're having trouble closing the sale, you probably need to work on the "front stage" part of your process—those visible qualities that engage the buyer.

If you have ever dined at a fine restaurant and then been invited back to the kitchen to meet the staff that prepared it, you know that what happens behind the scenes to produce an outstanding meal is usually messy. This kind of "backstage view" should only be shared with the customer for specific reasons, such as to honor the gratitude of an especially interested or loyal patron.

The front stage of your conversion process is a show—a series of carefully orchestrated activities designed to further engage your prospective customer and allow you to best serve them. When I started my landscape business I met my residential clients at their home or a coffee shop because the start-up team was using every inch of space in my overcrowded home office. However, when we moved into our new building, a key aspect of our process was to hold the introductory client meeting in our office conference room. This enabled buyers to meet several of our team members, notice our awards and beautiful framed projects hanging on the walls, and to otherwise conclude that we indeed were a professional business capable of doing much more than just meeting their needs. The most important part was the physical act of them coming to our office. It made the first meeting an event, one in which we were prepared to introduce our process, which was prominently on display as a graphic representation of the essential steps.

Indeed, that was the meeting's true objective—not to sell products but to sell the process for creating whatever they could imagine. This is the essence of designing your business for relevance in a customer-driven environment. The old mindset was the business finding customers for their products and services. The new one is collaborating with the customers whose trust you have earned to develop better products and services for them.

It just so happened that the essential steps in our design-sales process all began with the letter C: Communication, Collaboration, Creativity, and Commitment. The initial no-obligation get-together was the Communication Meeting.

If the potential customer chose to move forward, we then held the Collaboration Meeting, one in which we all worked together from intentionally rough sketches we had prepared in advance to create a springboard for launching new ideas.

The third gathering was the Creativity Meeting. This was where we sought to "wow" the customer with the three best preliminary master designs our architects had created, based on what we learned at the previous meeting. There was nearly always one that jumped off the table, with the best elements of the others being incorporated into it to create the final plan. Of course, we discussed budgets at every meeting. We began with a wide range that narrowed as we progressed through our process to the final meeting—that was appropriately called the Commitment Meeting. It was therefore clear from the beginning that if we did our job well, we expected a financial commitment at that meeting. This was usually less of a meeting and more a celebration of what everyone was excited about—getting started transforming their outdoor environment into something special.

While your sales process will differ from ours, it will very likely include an initial "discovery" meeting to help both sides determine if there is a potentially good fit that merits moving forward together. Beyond that you will have to design your process according to practices necessary to achieve your desired outcomes. Read further and you will learn that contrary to what many may think, the sales process is not linear, but ideally circular to better serve and retain your customers.

YOUR BACKSTAGE PROCESS

When you set clear expectations for your customers, you put them at ease and dramatically increase your rate of closing new business—and keeping it sold. Nobody likes surprises, and you can eliminate the majority of them by accurately and honestly describing what is going to (or supposed to) happen next. That is something I have attempted to do in this book. A lot of experts might tell you it is easy to use social media to grow your business—which is quite possibly why so many businesses give up just as they are about to achieve what they rightfully earned.

You usually want to hide the behind-the-scenes happenings from the customer, because business—especially small business—is messy in the trenches. You know this as a small-business person yourself; however, it may not be quite as evident to someone who has worked their entire career in a corporate environment. It was certainly a wake-up call for me when I made the transition. This is why it is easier for one small business person to sell to another; they understand the challenges, and thus respect when others get it right.

You can seriously increase your business's growth potential by focusing on a single component of your process that other companies often ignore or compromise. Specifically, you want to integrate the back end of your process into the beginning to make the entire process circular—and do it with your most talented people. A thank-you note to close out a transaction isn't enough anymore. Arrange a call or meeting to discuss with your customer how you can further enhance their situation—and take that opportunity to show them how you can do even more. Better yet, ask them how they think you can do so.

Think about what often happens at the close of a business transaction. In many cases, you complete a survey to share your thoughts with the company. It's all about the seller. Isn't it better to focus on the customer to make sure everything is working properly—and fix it if it isn't? If your business is seeking more favorable comments on social channels, this is an ideal way to encourage them. However, you should always consider earning those comments as a backstage activity that becomes an unexpected surprise if it happens. The customer shouldn't feel obligated to do so.

NAME YOUR PROCESS

I refined my landscape process while I was involved with The Strategic Coach, a focusing program for entrepreneurs with locations in the United States, Canada, and the United Kingdom. The program's founder, Dan Sullivan, teaches the magic of naming your business process. When you put a name on something, it becomes your own. It makes it unique to your business, and therefore invaluable for differentiating the business in competitive markets.

Branding is not usually associated with small business. However, we're now living in a world where consumers don't always trust companies, and become easily frustrated with poor service. It can therefore be powerful to have a branded process that gives your buyers confidence in the fact that you have thoroughly organized your business to serve them well.

In case you are curious, the name of our process was The Intelligent Landscape System™. It was actually a play on words—that we took an intelligent approach, and that we also respected the Intelligence of Nature and sought to work with her to create something for our clients that was not only beautiful, but sustainable, too.

Naming your process is as simple as starting with the word "The" to indicate it is uniquely singular—followed by a descriptive word or phrase—and then adding a technological or scientific word such as system, method, or process.

SALES AND MARKETING CONGRUENCY

When I was studying business in school, our textbooks taught us about the inherent incongruences between sales, marketing, and production. We learned to expect conflict between these departments: marketing making promises that sales cannot keep, or production failing to stock sufficient inventory to meet market demands in an attempt to manage their costs more efficiently.

This is just one example of how much business has changed—at least, how I hope it has. If there is friction within a company, the customer is going to learn about it soon enough and seek another company to work with. They will especially be sensitive to any incongruence between marketing and sales. This is why it's wise to involve your salespeople in your social marketing planning and implementation; both sales and social marketing are the voice of your business—one team, one voice.

I once read that every question during a job interview can be distilled down to three essential questions to which every candidate must be able to effectively and affirmatively respond; you want the job, you can handle the job, and we'll enjoy working with you. This applies equally for acquiring new business, and therefore can serve as a guide to focus your relationship selling efforts. Let's look at each component in more detail.

YOUR COMPANY WANTS THE BUSINESS

Your marketing should clearly indicate that you are in business for a profit, and that you want more business opportunities. Failing to do so places an additional burden on the sales team, whose job should be as simple as taking warm leads and guiding them through the remaining steps of the sales process. In other words, selling today is more relationship management than anything else.

Some business people believe that being overly enthusiastic is a sign of an amateur. But what customer wouldn't want to work with a business that's excited to have their patronage?

It's not a sign of an amateur at all; rather, it's a signal to the customer that this company is going to put all of their energy into solving their problems before, during, and after the sale. In fact, I've discovered that enthusiasm is one of the best qualities for inexperienced salespeople that are still building their skills. Sometimes that alone is enough to earn the buyer's trust.

When I interviewed job candidates I was always attracted to those that showed a great deal of enthusiasm for joining our team. I knew that first impressions are an indication of what will follow. The way that you introduce your company to buyers should be congruent across all aspects of your sales and marketing. We accomplished this by training everyone in our company on our process. Today, that would also be reflected in our social media.

You may wonder: Is it possible to want the business too much? How many phone calls or e-mails are too many? I was always curious about this myself. I took an approach that is consistent with the culture of social media: you can keep asking, but you must also keep adding value. Try to contribute something useful every time you connect with a customer, whether in person or using social media. This, combined with your enthusiasm, clearly suggests your intentions for helping them. And according to LinkedIn co-founder Reid Hoffman, you should persist until you get either a yes or a no. Some people are busy and will respond only when the time is right for them; so be persistent.

YOU CAN HANDLE THE BUSINESS

Your social marketing is especially well suited to helping your communities understand that your company has the credentials, expertise, and experience to capably handle their business. Stories that illustrate how your company delivered exceptional experiences for your customers helps others see their circumstances in those situations—thereby compelling them to engage with your business.

Testimonial letters are not evidence that you can handle the business any more than positive ratings on Yelp, Foursquare, or Facebook are. Though these can help, they are not definitive; they're only suggestions of your potential. This is why it is helpful to pull back the curtain to reveal details that are undeniable evidence that could not possibly be fabricated. Contextual examples are more likely to move a buyer to action, especially when they are persuasively delivered by one of your delighted customers.

Consumers are becoming more media-savvy, and therefore getting better at sniffing out five-star social media ratings that have evidently been posted by friends. It's up to you and your sales team to get on the same page by understanding and sharing your best stories, which ideally should be captured on your blog so they are just a click away. That's right, stories are the best testimonial because they are shareable, and that makes them powerful social objects for promoting your business.

THEY WILL ENJOY WORKING WITH YOU

Being easy to work with is the hallmark of a business that values each and every one of its customers, and treats them accordingly. Once again, it matters more what the customers say than the business. So, always be ready with camera and camcorder to record live situations in your business environment with real customers. It will be even more credible if you don't try to make the finished product overly polished or staged.

Social media amplifies all of our human qualities, so use it well to show the personality of your business. When I visited the Zappos headquarters I observed how employees had decorated their individual offices with streamers, balloons, and beads—just about anything you could imagine. It was clear that Zappos doesn't just tolerate self-expression; they encourage it. My favorite cubicle was a prominent one along the hallway that had a shrine to musician Rick Springfield, best known for his number one hit song, *Jessie's Girl*.

One of Zappos' core values is being a little weird. While that may not necessarily work in your business environment, it is safe to say that most people want to have fun and will appreciate this as one aspect of doing business with you. Most people that have flown Southwest Airlines know they do everything they can to make flying with them a feel-good experience, even when something goes wrong. Business is now personal, and that means companies need to loosen up a little to show their customers they have permission to do the same.

RELATIONSHIP SELLING PRACTICES

The following practices are some that you will find especially useful for converting engagement into new business—online, offline, and on the telephone.

Talk in the Future

One of the advantages of a well-designed sales process is it helps your customers visualize where you are taking them, and the steps you will be following to get there. Therefore, one thing that helps to close more business is to speak freely about the future. However, if you notice that despite your efforts your buyer is having trouble imagining a future with your business, it may be better to graciously take a pass and move on.

One of our company's policies was to never end a meeting without scheduling the next. The idea was to keep the process moving into the future, which presumably was where we all wanted to go together. When your buyer is talking about a future with your business, you know you are doing the right things in the present moment.

Build Value Before Budgets

There inevitably comes a time when you have to talk pricing or budgets to make a sale. If your content marketing and social media engagement efforts have done their job well, the interested buyer will ask—and you want to wait as long as necessary for that to happen. If they don't, it's a sign that you have not created sufficient value.

I have been on the phone with clients inquiring about my services for days before they asked about fees. This opens up more space to add value. If you start talking price too soon, it only means the business is ready to close—and that could end the discussions. So as difficult as it can be sometimes—wait for the buyer. It will pay off in the long run.

Offer Choices

Consumers love to have choices, but it is the job of your social marketing and sales process to narrow down those choices to just a few. Too many choices is confusing for people, and usually results in them making no decision at all. In other words, a confused mind says no.

In the years ahead, marketing and sales will be nearly indistinguishable. This will come as a direct result of the value that content marketing brings to consumers for making better buying decisions.

The power of search makes it possible for anyone to curate extensive lists of choices, but in our risk-averse economy people want help narrowing down that list to the best choices. That's where any business can shine—by applying experience and expertise to helping buyers that don't know what they do. For example, as a landscape professional I knew that there were hundreds of varieties of crabapple trees available, and they were all beautiful. Do you know how many were disease resistant? Less than a dozen. It was therefore my responsibility to only present those choices to my customers.

Don't Oversell

While it's not amateurish to be enthusiastic, amateurs are notorious for overselling. They overwhelm their buyer with so much information that it becomes impossible to make a decision. Experience teaches you to look for signals that the buyer is ready. One is asking the price.

Another is placing a wallet or checkbook in sight. When a client walked into our Commitment Meeting and placed their checkbook on the table, we knew we were done selling. We simply allowed everyone to get settled in before moving into the details of closing the sale.

Respond to Social Signals

Social signals in face-to-face selling situations are subtle clues that your buyer is ready to close the deal. Some positive social signals are future-based comments or questions, such as "What's next?" This indicates that your buyer is ready to move forward with you; so don't keep them waiting a minute longer. Of course, there are negative social signals, too—like inattention, impatience, and closed body language such as crossed arms—these, too, you must acknowledge and respond to, otherwise you have reached an impasse.

DESIGNING YOUR SALES PROCESS

Entrepreneurs who launch a company either find a way to make it work, or move on to something else. The entrepreneurial work ethic is what enabled many of us to make it through those difficult early years. I recall many days where I started out at 5 a.m. and didn't get home until late at night. But you get smarter after awhile, and before long you find your stride—until you're facing the next obstacle or economic downturn.

The methods and procedures that get a small business through the early years often develop as a result of practices and habits that are unique to the owner. You will find your process embedded within those practices if you take the time to study it and break it down step-by-step.

In other words, you can begin to build your sales conversion process by mentally revisiting your biggest successes and writing down exactly what was involved in making those successes. Chances are you will begin to notice patterns and the key steps of your process will be associated with them. These patterns will usually be activities that made something better—easier, faster, more enjoyable—all of the experiences customers desire. Write them down, give them a name, and then share them with your team to see if they agree.

Then test this sales process on the work before you now. Are you doing everything the way you used to? Look at some of your recent failures. Did you skip some of the steps that previously worked well for you? Unless they're written down you're likely to miss critical steps from time to time.

There is always the temptation to move quickly when you see the finish line; however, that can compromise the result. If you are like the rest of us, you will never forget your biggest blunders—and that remembered pain is usually what keeps you from repeating them.

Conversely, time has a way of erasing the memory of the good habits that served us well while we were growing our businesses. Have you stopped planning as much as you used to? Do you find you are doing more business over the phone than you had once done face-to-face? These changes can compromise the effectiveness of your natural process—and cost you sales.

During the early days of my landscape business we used sub-contractors to perform the work that was beyond the capabilities of our crews. By the time we developed our Intelligent Landscape System™ we had eliminated most subcontractors to better control our schedules and the quality of work we delivered.

One day, I was building a list of the most profitable projects in the history of our company so that we could learn what made them so successful. It became apparent that during the early years using more subcontractors kept our overhead low. Thus, it was clear that it was necessary to rethink the current process and consider using more subcontractors again, while also applying our acquired experience for choosing those that would best mesh with our improved system.

DESIGN YOUR PROCESS AROUND THE NEW CUSTOMER

What got you here isn't going to get you to the next level—at least, not with all of the changes taking place in the business environment. When you consider the convergence of social's influences, the new economic conditions, and the ongoing changes in technology, you have a perfect storm developing that is ripe for disrupting many industries.

We talked in Chapter 2 about how the influences of social media have significantly altered consumer behaviors, expectations and, as a result, the success criteria for most businesses. Apple opened its first retail store in London in late 2004, which happened to coincide nicely with the beginnings of social media. Did they foresee the trend or just get lucky?

It is staggering to consider the effects of social, local, and mobile that are sweeping over us right now, and how they will alter what works in the marketplace. If I still operated my landscape business today, I imagine we would be using Skype to replace or supplement some of those standard meetings.

I'm also sure we would be using cloud computing to share documents with customers in real time. And I'm certain we would not only be using video, but would probably have a relationship with a local videographer because video is destined to become important for social marketing success for small businesses.

It's safe to say I would be sitting down with my team on at least an annual basis to reexamine the essential steps of our business processes, and most especially the social marketing process that we have covered in these nine chapters.

Examining all of your business processes to better design them around the customer will prove to be vital for avoiding the race to the bottom—which is the subject of the next and final chapter.

Try This: Refine Your Sales Process

Either by yourself, or preferably together with your sales team, list your 20 favorite projects, transactions, or sales experiences.

- Organize them as you see fit. Consider variables such as:
  - Profitability
  - Customer Satisfaction
  - Repeat Business
  - Referrals
- Now determine what specifically happened that made these sales events exceptional. Did they include:
  - More time interviewing the buyer?
  - Engaging the buyer with current customers?
  - Setting expectations in advance?
  - A team approach?
  - Asking specific questions?
- Use the results of this analysis to refine and rewrite your sales process into its most essential elements. Focus on your front stage process and the backstage details will naturally follow from it.

CHAPTER 10

Avoiding the Race
to the Bottom

JUST SHOW UP

Social marketing is not going to do anything for you that you were not already capable of doing. If your business is broken now, this isn't going to fix it. However, if you have the right intentions it can help you develop what you need to get and keep your business moving forward.

As you now know, my small business succeeded because of my initial ignorance of generally accepted industry practices. I may have never taken the plunge had I known at the outset what I later learned.

The same holds true with social media. Fortunately, we can all look back on our experiences with gratitude. The memories and stories about our victories and failures are all part of our learning curve, and they make our day-to-day work that much more interesting.

You have a great deal of enthusiasm for your business and how you serve your customers—that much I know because

I cannot recall meeting a small business owner that didn't. When you bring that energy to this social marketing platform it becomes the magic that makes everything possible.

YOUR WORK IS NEVER DONE

You have to look at your social marketing as a work in progress. As my client Bob often remarked—your work is never done. Done is an ending that means your business has stopped growing. That is a surefire way to achieve mediocrity—what Seth Godin calls the race to the bottom.

If you are a risk taker, as I suspect you are if you are reading this, then you know there is always more to do. You know that work is a gift, and that the world needs your contribution. As I see it, the risk is to join the club, because when you do that you are encouraged to think and behave just like the other members.

The race to the bottom is the result of our commercial and social systems trying to get us to fit in—don't do it. Once your work becomes a commodity you lose those unique qualities that social media amplifies.

If you are paying attention to the world around you, you already know that people get into ruts and never get out—their path through life keeps getting narrower. They fear changes such as social media that can open up new opportunities for them. Regrettably, there is not much we can do about it.

There are a lot of amazing people out there and you are one of them—but your customers won't know that unless you share what you know, with the social networks ideally suited for that. Give them that chance. Give yourself that opportunity. As Steve Jobs said in describing how he built one of the most respected businesses on the planet, "Once you learn the people around you are no smarter than you are, you can change the world." That mindset enabled him to innovate and achieve greatness, and it's one that will give you the confidence to navigate the inevitable technological changes that businesses are sure to encounter in the years ahead.

There are people out there who know a lot more about technology than you do; yet they cannot seem to grasp the simple concept of digital social graphs that I've shared with you in this book. It just makes sense that connections lead to more connections, and sharing leads to better relationships, and relationships not only build trust—they build businesses that are winning the race to the top.

Winning the race to the top is really quite simple—take the risk of innovating. Design a better way—one that will delight your customers. Trust your understanding of your customers, work together to create what they may have never imagined was possible, and then take the steps to make it reality.

It starts with you.

HOW THIS WORKS

Does this really work? It's a question I'm often asked.

During the early days of blogging we were all just trying to figure out where new media was going. I would write about whatever was on my mind on a particular day, and often record a short video to accompany it. I wrote about business, but used everyday stories ranging from my son's interactions with Halloween trick-or-treaters to the creative methods colleges used to attract top students, such as one that secured my daughter's attendance at Indiana University's Kelley School of Business.

Anyway, one day I was riffing off a poem in my head that I learned during my days of teaching meditation when working with Deepak Chopra and his organization, something I did while concurrently operating my landscape business. The words were from Rumi, a Persian poet believed to have lived during the 13th century AD.

Rumi said, "When I die I will soar with the Angels, and when I die as an Angel, what I will become you cannot imagine." That's what I began typing into my blog post. Then I followed that thought to suggest that this fascinating new thing we called social media was just like that. It was soaring and going places, but where it would take us we could not imagine.

PRESS PUBLISH

A few months after publishing that, I received a call from a speakers bureau that had been searching the web for a small business social media speaker. After learning about the bureau's client I was reasonably confident we had a fit and encouraged her to recommend me.

She asked where my online videos were hosted so that her client could see me in action. At the time I did not have a traditional demo video online—only on a DVD. "You must have something," she said. I suggested the client could review the videos on my blog. That's when I first realized the power of blogging for building an extensive body of work online.

"Great," she responded. "I'll just send them to your blog." A few days later I learned her client wanted me to be the key-note speaker for their annual conference—and they wanted me to build a program around the idea expressed in that Rumi post—where social media is going you cannot imagine, but businesses clearly need to learn more about it if they expect to keep their marketing relevant.

That single blog post that I considered to be a throw-away piece resulted in a relationship with that bureau, multiple bookings with that client, as well as with others, future speaking engagements with related associations, new relationships with other bureaus, and so on.

ENJOY THE PROCESS

If I connect the dots I can trace that single blog post to over six figures of income. Yes, this indeed works, but how it happens is unpredictable. You have to simply get in the game, start at the logical beginning, do the work, and of course, follow a reliable process.

What's interesting is I never started blogging to accomplish anything in particular. I didn't have any great expectations. I just enjoyed it and found myself doing it for the simple reason that I could.

It was thrilling to push that publish button and wonder who I might connect with next. The possibilities are infinite—and that is the amazing power that social media gives us when we just put a few simple actions into practice.

Over time some nice things started happening, such as having my blog ranked one of the top small business blogs in the world, landing the deal for this book, and being here now to share what I've learned to help you grow your business.

Anyone can do this. My advantage was simply enjoying the process of sharing so much that I wanted to keep doing it again. It's a privilege. I will promise you that you will indeed get results that will exceed your expectations. You will discover talents you never knew. And you will open doors that have been closed; you just won't know when or where until you get there.

More than anything, you will discover the artist within you, and also within the new connections you make. This will open your eyes to possibilities around you that were previously unseen.

One of the things meditation teaches us is that we are all connected. Social media proves that to be true, and social marketing makes your business better for it. You just have to build it into your standard business practices.

Everyone is just one connection from a new breakthrough, provided they are willing to take the risk of using these techniques to plant the seeds of new possibilities. As the first lesson in the Introduction suggests, just show up—get started—and learn as you go.

Then write or connect with me on social media to let me know about your successes—or just to say hello. More on how to do that in the Appendix.

Appendix: Online Resources

WEB PAGE FOR THIS BOOK

Here you'll find articles, contests, interviews, and other valuable resources (including how to interview Jeff for your blog):

www.jeffkorhan.com/built-in-social

CHAPTER MENTIONS

Chapter One

- *How to Protect Your Facebook Account from Hackers:*

  www.jeffkorhan.com/2011/08/how-to-protect-your-facebook-account-from-hackers.html

Chapter Two

- *Ford Fiesta Video:*

  http://youtu.be/4TshFWSsrn8

Chapter Three

- *Why Marketers Are Now in the Answers Business:*
  www.jeffkorhan.com/2011/12/marketers-answers-business.html

Chapter Four

- *LinkedIn Blog:*
  http://blog.linkedin.com

- *Facebook Blog:*
  https://blog.facebook.com

- *Twitter Blog:*
  http://blog.twitter.com

- *Official Google Blog:*
  http://googleblog.blogspot.com

Chapter Seven

- *QR Codes Save Lives (the stop afib story and links to other QR code articles):*
  www.jeffkorhan.com/2012/10/qr-codes-save-lives.html

- *John Butterill Google+ Hangout Video:*
  www.youtube.com/watch?v=y1Uv7as5ZmI

- *LinkedIn InMaps Video:*
  www.youtube.com/watch?v=PC99Nw2JX8w

Chapter Eight

- *Resources on blogging, content marketing, and using Google Reader:*

  www.jeffkorhan.com/content-marketing

CONNECT WITH JEFF KORHAN

- *Primary website for Jeff Korhan:*

  www.jeffkorhan.com

- *Hire Jeff to speak:*

  www.jeffkorhan.com/professionally-speaking

- *Subscribe to Jeff's newsletter:*

  www.jeffkorhan.com/newsletter

- *Follow Jeff on Twitter:*

  https://twitter.com/jeffkorhan

- *Connect with Jeff on LinkedIn:*

  http://linkedin.com/in/jeffkorhan

- *Join Jeff's Facebook page community:*

  http://on.fb.me/9TJ5Lf

- *Circle Jeff on Google+:*

  www.gplus.to/jeffkorhan

Acknowledgments

Thank you to everyone who made this book possible. Since this is a business book, that includes everyone who I have worked with—and that has contributed in some way to my work. I would especially like to thank Steve Camp, Cynthia Fletcher, and Eric Tharp. It was a privilege working with you in the small business trenches.

Also, Seth Godin, Chris Brogan, Brian Clark, Brian Solis, Michael Stelzner, John Jantsch, Guy Kawasaki, Mari Smith, Deepak Chopra, Bill Dean, Chakrapani Ullal, Dan Sullivan, Zig Ziglar, Al Lautenslager, Kevin O'Connor, Patty Allen, Andrea Gold, and of course, Leslie and my parents.

Special thanks to Randall Craig, Marty Grunder, Linda Dessau, and Alison Korhan for reviewing chapters and providing ideas and fresh perspectives, and Bruce BecVar for your inspiring music.

And the team at Wiley—Lauren Murphy for supporting this project from start to finish, Christine Moore for pushing me to make it better, and Deborah Schindlar for bringing it home.

Index

INDEX

INDEX

INDEX